Your College Experience

Your College Experience

How To Tackle Each and Every Day of College Head On

ALLISON KATHLEEN
VANSAGHI

For my parents, Heather and Mark Vansaghi,
who gave me the opportunity to attend college and
grow into the bold individual I am today, thank you.

CONTENTS

INTRODUCTION

A Little Bit About Me

Hello, everyone! First, I want to start out by saying thank you for taking the time to read what I have written. This is my first book, and it is truly an honor that you are all reading it. **My name is Allison Vansaghi, and I am a completely average recent college graduate student.** I graduated from Rowan University, a university in Glassboro, New Jersey. After dabbling with a few major choices, I finished with a Communication Studies degree. Recently, after having grown up in a shore town in New Jersey, I learned to adapt to city life in Philadelphia. In terms of my college experience, nothing about me necessarily stands out. I wrote this book so you could hear college advice from someone who actually went through it rather than hearing advice from someone who may never have gotten the chance to experience college.

This book is raw: I cover pretty much everything you'll be thinking about during your time in college, things you'll want to know before you start, and things you'll enjoy revisiting if you have already graduated. During the months after my graduation, I really enjoyed reflecting on my time at Rowan. I wish I had had something like this book to read when I was going through college! It's my greatest wish that I can help you guys out a little bit. I hope you find humor and also truth in this book.

Keep in mind that these lessons are from personal experience and that every college story varies. You may agree with what I say … or you might disagree. Just keep an open mind, buckle up, and enjoy this rollercoaster of a book. Most of all, good luck with your endeavors and the start of something new!

PART ONE
WELCOME HOME

CHAPTER 1

The First Day

It's the day you've been waiting for ever since you learned what was in store for you after four years of your dreadful high school saga. You've spent the last six months looking up videos titled "A day in the life of a [fill in the blank] student." You've been applying to schools you knew you'd never go to, but you've been picturing your life changing in the Appalachian mountains, anyway. You've been imagining how you'll move in next to the cute boy/girl you've seen in your dreams. And of course you'll also immediately decide what you want to be for the rest of your life.

At this point, it feels like your life is about to change forever—and believe me, it will. You will learn life lessons in college that you will revisit throughout your entire life. You will make lifelong friends and completely recreate yourself. There will be hard times, but you will find your inner strength and overcome them. You will find that by the end of this whole journey, you will be a completely different person than you are right now. College is your canvas, you have the power to paint any picture you desire.

Just as yours will be, my freshman year was a rollercoaster of events. You are plummeting into a whole new world and trying to keep a grip on everything around you. It will be pleasant at times; it will also feel impossible at times. Just like a rollercoaster ride has exciting parts—parts when you are scared and parts when you are just coasting along—so will your college experience. At times, it will feel like a dream that you never want to wake up from. Then there will be other times when you'll feel like you would rather be *anywhere* else but where you are in that moment. Just keep this in mind: **we are in this together, and ultimately, you will come out of school as the best version of yourself.** The biggest thing you need to remember going into your first day is that everyone else around you is scared, too. No one knows what to expect at this point. Although you may be terrified, you will adapt to your new home more quickly than you expect to.

Moving In and Meeting Your Roommate

It's happening so fast! Your dad is out of breath because he just carried 100+ pounds of your stuff that you couldn't live without up to the third floor of a 200-year-old building while your mom can't keep her tears in. You finally manage to cram the wholesale lug of snacks your mom insisted you take into an extremely small double room next to your bins of clothing, stacks of notebooks, and a mini fridge. Just then, your unfamiliar roommate walks in with *their* 100-pound amount of must-haves. At this moment, you have no idea how close the two of you will get, whether you like it or not.

As the two of you finally fit in all of the items you need to feel at home Tetris-style, it finally hits you that you've made it. You're there. It's time to say goodbye to the people who have worked so hard to get you where you are now. Suddenly, a few hour's drive away or a few states away feels like worlds away. Although you're ready, you're scared.

You will eventually become comfortable living on your own, but here's my first big life tip: don't ever forget who helped you get to college. All too often, college students forget to appreciate their parents after moving on to adulthood, but your parents/guardians worked extremely hard to set you up for an amazing future. Always appreciate them and tell them you love them every chance you get.

Your roommate will either be someone you avoid at all costs or someone who provides serious support during your first year. With so much going on in that first year of school, whether you like to admit it or not, you guys will need each other. You will most likely spend nights getting to know each other and will look to each other for guidance on certain things. My roommate and I went through our ups and downs, yelling at each other when we were stressed and then hugging each other when we went through bad times. But not all of us can be this lucky—sometimes roommate situations go from bad to worse.

If you are dealing with a bad roommate this early into college, I am sorry for you. It can feel like one of the worst things in the world. Your first room in college is meant to feel like a home away from home, and if there's someone getting in the way of that, it can be a torturous experience. That said, agreeing to a random roommate is sometimes a risk you have to take. Fortunately for me, I was paired with someone who eventually ended up being one of my closest friends. Sure, we had our differences, but in the end, we were roommates and we had each other's back.

When it comes to roommates, keep a positive mindset, respect each other's space, and always show kindness. Hopefully your room-mate will do the same for you. If you are still having a hard time with your roommate, remember that the year will eventually be over and you'll never have to talk to them again. Be strong through this. I have seen how hard it can be to deal with a less-than-ideal roommate situation. Just know that if your roommate isn't provid-ing support for you, they are only one of the thousand-plus students on your campus. Your roommate does not have to be your best friend—you will meet other people very soon.

Your First Day . . . and Night

The first day is consumed with moving in, making small talk with your new roommate, and going over your class schedule over and over again to make sure you DO NOT walk into the wrong class-room. Somehow we all make that mistake at least once in our col-lege careers, so don't get too upset when it happens to you. All of the classrooms tend to look alike, after all—it is not far-fetched that you will mix up the room numbers. You might even continue to make this mistake in your senior year.

Do not be afraid to make mistakes in your first few weeks. You will quickly learn that no one really cares about that kind of stuff like they did in high school. Somehow, those few months between senior year of high school and freshman year of college bring about a sense of maturity—not many people in college care about what you wear or the minor mistakes you make. Walking into the wrong classroom or wearing the wrong outfit at times will be the least of your worries. You'll soon learn that the universal wardrobe in college consists of sweatpants and a stained t-shirt, anyway.

The sun sets quickly. Before you know it, your first night of college has arrived. Everyone you knew before entering this black hole of adulthood plans to meet up to slug Four Lokos and cram into a completely unsafe, moist environment that becomes pretty fun for you...*at least, for a few years.* For now, these moldy basements that smell of beer and regret begin to shape your college existence. The highlight of going to class during freshman year is meeting other freshmen who also enjoy basement beer parties.

Making Friends

You may not know anyone right away, and that's okay, too. **You are not meant to have your high school friends magically end up at the same school where you end up.** I was fortunate to have a few people I knew from high school around during my freshman year, and spending time with them helped me make friends pretty quickly. But know that there is no timeline to making friends or finding your group of people. Do not stress if this doesn't happen for you right away. **The beauty of freshman dorms is that everyone is all kind of lost together.** You'll find that everyone starts to leak out of their rooms that are so uncomfortably close to yours, looking for others who are just as nervous as they are. Being social isn't always for everyone, but you owe it to yourself to get out there and make some friends. Like I said before, you are not the only one scared at this point, I promise.

These friends can become lifelong best friends or just people who introduce you to other groups of friends. The beginning of college is everyone basically feeling out who they get along with best. It will most likely take some time to find the people you are comfortable with. It may seem frightening to feel like you haven't found your group, but you will. Do not be afraid to stop hanging around people who make you uncomfortable.

Also know that some friends are temporary—not everyone is meant to be in your life forever. Although I still cherish the times I had with some of my friends in college, it is completely normal to drift apart. It can hurt when it's happening, but remember, if someone wants to stay in your life, they will.

Also remember that you will always end up right where you are supposed to be. It might take a little longer sometimes, but in the end, it will be worth it. Whereas during high school you were confined to a smaller group of people for four years, college is a time to find people who compliment your style. Take advantage of this freedom! Although it may be occasionally hard to get out there—you'll need to figure out different ways that work for you—you will find your way eventually. Finding people who allow you to be yourself at all times is just a part of the process.

You will meet a lot of people your first year in college. Always be yourself. That way, you'll know that your group of people really *is* for you, and knowing that will save you trouble in the long run. Finding friends in college is all about supporting each other and making the experience just a little bit more enjoyable.

Some Essential Supplies

If you are the first person in your family to go to college, there are a few essential purchases you should consider making before arriving. By this time, you have already been dealing with things like the FAFSA and sorting out everything else your parents really knew nothing about. Once you have finally figured out how to do all of that, though, you may be neglecting further necessities that you'll need once you get to school. You may be thinking, "But college is expensive already! I really have to buy more things before I get there?" While nothing I list below is an absolute necessity, you could bring just a few things with you to make your life easier once you are a full-time student.

#1 A Laptop

Purchasing a laptop might be out of your and your family's price range—laptops are not cheap. *But* it's possible to finance laptops. This is a great option and can also do great things for your credit. Your computer will be where everything is saved; essentially, it's like a binder without all of the weight. Great platforms are available for keeping all of your notes and assignments in one place so that you don't have to worry about losing them. Thankfully, we are part of the great advancement that is technology. I suggest you take advantage of this.

A laptop will allow you to take notes in class more efficiently, because although in high school your teachers may have talked slowly enough for you to be able to take full notes by hand, your college professors will proceed more quickly through the lessons. Also, a computer will allow you to purchase virtual textbooks, work on assignments anywhere you are, and make sure that you're organized. Going to the library to use their computers will become a pain real fast. **If you plan on only purchasing one thing for college, I suggest you try to get a laptop.**

#2 Headphones

You can find a good pair of headphones for pretty cheap nowadays. College is a loud place in general (even in the library), but headphones will block out any unwanted noise so you can study in peace. You will also want a pair to use in the gym and while walking to class so you don't have to say hi to everyone you pass. That probably seems like a rude idea, but believe me, you'll understand this advantage in a few weeks. Besides, even though headphones don't seem like something you will necessarily need, some classes require you to have them. **Finding a cheap pair of headphones isn't necessarily a bad idea. However, investing in a good pair will prevent you from having to buy multiple pairs.**

#3 An Umbrella and a Raincoat

If you plan on walking to class or walking anywhere, rain gear is something you should highly consider. There is nothing worse than walking to or from class just when it starts to rain. If you are unprepared, rain will become your worst enemy, especially if you are walking to another class and not your dorm—sitting in class soaked like a wet dog can distract you from what matters. A raincoat and umbrella will keep you dry for the most part and is definitely worth purchasing.

#4 A Reusable Water Bottle

A reusable water bottle will save you money and will keep you from having to purchase cases of water. Cases of water are cheap, but depending on where you live, carrying them up to your dorm could be the worst. Nothing is worse than already being (debatably) late for class and realizing you drank your last water bottle the night before. By supplying yourself with a reusable water bottle, you'll always have water when you're going to class. More importantly than that, you won't have to carry cases of water into your dorm.

#5 Sturdy Shoes

Although you'll want to have nice shoes for more formal gatherings, you'll want to make sure you have a pair of shoes that you can beat up. Parties, day-longs, and everything in between will cause your shoes to accumulate a thick layer of *who knows what*. Make sure you designate a pair of shoes for informal gatherings that you won't be upset about messing up. You'll always want to have a pair for rainy days, events in the mud, etc.

#6 Mattress Pad

You would think that paying so much money for college would mean they would supply you with a comfy mattress. Sadly, the slab of dense, cement-like springs you'll be getting will not assist your sleeping in any way. To ensure that you will not experience back problems your first year of college, bring a mattress pad. It seems like a small thing, but your first night in your dorm will make you realize that *anything* on top of the mattress they give you is an improvement. Getting good sleep during your first year of college isn't easy to begin with, but a comfortable mattress will make this a little more achievable.

#7 A Planner

You will soon learn that mentally keeping track of all of your responsibilities becomes impossible. If you don't believe me, try it out the first week or two and see where you're at. Starting as early as your freshman year, to keep track of all of your classes and extra responsibilities, you'll need to write everything down—if you don't, you will absolutely forget about things. Having a planner will not only help with assignment deadlines, it will keep you from forgetting birthdays, event commitments, free time activities, work schedules, etc. Do yourself a favor and get a planner where you can write everything down. If it weren't for my planner, I would look like a fish out of water trying to manage my time—even in adulthood, a planner is a necessity. What's even more comical is in that your old age, a planner is something that excites you. You may even ask for a new one for Christmas or any holiday when you receive gifts. *Ah, the facts of getting old ...*

#8 Comfortable Clothes

Although you will eventually want to have clothes that express your style and prepare you for future interviews, you'll want to have a big collection of comfy clothes as well. I can guarantee that you are not going to want to put on jeans and a nice top for an 8 a.m. class. You are probably also not going to want to change out of what you slept in. Make sure that when you enter college, you have enough sweat-pants, t-shirts, and sweatshirts to last you a week or so. You may think that you will dress up for every class, but I can almost promise you that those dress-up clothes will start to collect dust in your closet. Everyone around you will be wearing what makes them comfortable. If "comfortable" means a sweat suit for you, make sure you have enough of them to not have to re-wear the same one throughout your whole college career.

There are definitely more items on my common list of must-haves, but the top few items I've listed here are things you should seriously consider acquiring before entering college. Each one of them will make your life easier. That said, college is a learning experience every day—very quickly, you will find out what you need and what you can live without. Set yourself up for an easier next few years and pay attention to the things that will help make your time in college more manageable.

CHAPTER 2

Freshman Year

Y OU'VE BEEN IN THIS FLU-/COLD-INFESTED environment for a few months now. Shared laundry rooms, freshman dining halls, student center hangouts, and being hungover in your 8 a.m. classes have become the norm. You've learned the hard way that dining hall sushi has a mind of its own, that the girls who wear the least amount of clothing get the most amount of attention, and that you're only cool if you can do a keg stand for more than 60 seconds.

And in addition to all that, you've learned that a lot of people around you seem like they know exactly what they want to do when they graduate. *They don't.* I mean, come on. Jenny came to college to be a dentist, and although she's been drunk every night since she arrived, she says she's going to graduate with a bio degree and go to medical school. And Jeremy from acting class might be the one with the drugs, but he says he's going for a business degree—he's going to be the chief marketing officer of a huge corporation. Here you were just trying to worry about having fun and adapting to your new home, but everyone around you can't seem to stop talking about their future. *Bleh.*

Chances are they are all obsessing over their career paths because they are trying to convince themselves that they have chosen the right path. College is a place where everyone is *supposed to* know where they want to end up, so bragging about it is the only way they can assure themselves that they are indeed doing the right thing. In a way, you can't blame them for trying to set themselves up for a bright future…but you also cannot let that stress you out. Keep reminding yourself that you are on your own timeline, not anyone else's.

NEWSFLASH: Not a single one of them actually knows exactly what they want to do, no matter how often they talk about it.

During our adolescent years, we were continuously pressured to move on to the next step, the next class, the next homework assignment. The issue of not knowing exactly what we want to do as young adults stems from having neglected spending time on our true passions at a young age. As adolescents, we were focusing on the piles of assignments that were due and the extra curriculars we signed up for and we were trying to figure out who we were academically. If we had been given more free time to focus on the things that made us happy and the things we were great at, then we would struggle less to choose a path during our young adult years.

The constant pressure we were under when we were young will not subside in our years to come. In a sense, this is where our role models have failed us. Our teachers, parents, sports coaches, etc. never really gave us a chance to catch our breath and spend time enjoying ourselves. So when you are incredibly stressed about choosing a path, keep in mind it is not your fault—on the contrary, society cared more about social studies and math than what you truly enjoyed doing. And people wonder why young adults all the way from age 18 through their late 20s feel lost about what we are good at, lost about what the right path to pursue is. Sure, we had electives in middle school and high school that gave us a short break from our core classes, but most of the time they were also required, and they only sparked our creativity for a short amount of time. To prepare for college, we were given the SATs and other standardized tests that determined how ready we were for the academic world ahead of us. Maybe if our role models had instead given us an assignment to find a new hobby, reflect on our talents, or review our aspirations, we wouldn't all change our college majors a handful of times.

I spent so much time during my adolescent years playing sports, trying to do well in school, and going through the motions that I never took a second to reflect on my talents. In school, we were always taught to never use "I" in our writing, so I never thought it was possible to succeed using the writing style I actually enjoyed. My writing classes were dry, filled with research papers and SAT prompts. I never even acknowledged my love for writing because it was masked by guidelines and what was grammatically correct. I wasn't the best at language arts or English, so I assumed that being an author was not in the cards for me.

A ton of high school students feel discouraged about particular subjects, and that feeling carries them through the next steps in their lives. If your teacher told you that writing wasn't your strong suit, you would never consider pursuing a career involving writing; if you weren't great in math, you would never consider being an engineer. But here's the truth: when you are thinking about your career choices, dreams, or life goals, remember that you can follow any path you set your mind to following. It sounds cliché, but you really *can* do anything you want to do. If you really care about something, try to do it every single day. If you keep yourself motivated and continuously remind yourself that you are capable of pursuing your passion, you will achieve anything you want to achieve.

This world gives us a lot more freedom than high school made it seem like we would have. If you want to be an author and write a book using "I" in every sentence, do it. There is no longer anyone stopping you from applying your creative passions. If your art teacher graded one of your projects as being poor, pick up a paintbrush and paint! There will most likely be someone out there who thinks your artwork is worth thousands. Put the strict guidelines from high school in the past. If your teachers didn't see your potential, prove them wrong and follow your dreams.

Another dream I had at a young age was to produce music. In college, I spent thousands in saved-up money to get myself lessons, equipment, and software. I had no idea where to start. I didn't know any music theory and I had never even seen the software I needed to use. I wanted to learn so badly, but I had never had enough money to go to school to study music theory. I spent time on it every single day, watched videos, practiced, tried different things out. I am still in the process of learning how exactly everything works.

To keep myself going, I remind myself of where I started and how far I have come since the first song I tried to make. There have been frustrating nights, times when I've wanted to throw my computer at the wall, and times when I almost gave up. But what I need to remember and what you also need to know is this: applying yourself to something you want to learn will eventually result in success. Do not look at something you know nothing about and assume you will never be able to learn it. Surprise yourself! Give something your all and believe in your capabilities. Determination and passion will show you that you are capable of achieving just about anything.

All that said, young adults face the harsh reality that we are expected to *know exactly* what we want to do for the rest of our life at far too young of an age. Society is putting extreme pressure on us to pick what we are good at, to choose one singular degree route that is going to make us internally happy, and then make a huge amount of income. College students are just becoming confident enough to express themselves through edgy combat boots and band tees, yet at the same time, they are expected to choose lifelong career paths!

The message that I wish my 18-year-old self would have gotten is this: society's expectation for us to know exactly what we want to do the second we enter college is *wrong*. Don't they understand that you are trying to focus on losing the Freshman 15 that came on faster than you thought? That you are just trying to get through Comp 1, sneak your car onto campus, and deal with a hundred other first-world problems? It's completely understandable that you can't choose between education, criminal justice, and psychology right now.

As a recent college graduate, I have some other great news for you: **your college major does not limit you to any career.** I'm sure there have been a select few educated people who have told you this, but you do not have to believe them. Their gibberish is not going to stop your stress rash from acting up at night. It is not going to stop the fact that you'll fall asleep on your computer as you're reading "A Day in the Life of a Teacher/Doctor/Journalist" followed by another article saying "Do Not Become a Teacher/Doctor/Journalist if it's the Last Thing You Do." I'm here to tell you that any degree you choose will ultimately result in getting a job that you will eventually enjoy. It may take a few tries to find a career you like, but do not think that if you major in math you cannot end up being a police officer or a botanist. You'll always have more options to educate yourself in whatever field you desire. Think of your degree as being the baseline to any career. Once you have your degree, you can always find another way to do whatever you choose.

Your life is incredibly huge. Time may seem shortened and your four years of college may seem like the only time you have to decide on a career path, but the truth is, it's just the very beginning. Sure, some people will go to school for engineering, graduate, and get a high-paying entry-level engineering job. But there will also be people who graduate with a communication studies degree, travel for the next four years, teach English in a foreign country, bartend while they're doing it, and find a perfect career for themselves at age 28.

Your journey changes by the day, and although you have absolutely no idea where your ride is headed, you need to trust that whatever the situation, you will figure it out. You may figure it out two years after you graduate college, when you're doing a summer internship on a cruise ship to Alaska. You may figure it out bartending at a nightclub, when you meet the CEO of Urban Outfitters. Or you may figure it out when you come back from a five-year stint in Hawaii. **Your journey of figuring things out should be more about the endless surprises along the way and less about the end result.** Alan Watts shares his knowledge when he stresses that **life should be about the dance, not the destination.** He explains that maybe we should look at life as more of a musical thing and just dance instead of constantly worrying about what comes next.

If you are overly concerned about the end result, you will miss the beauty in what is going on around you. We were not put on this Earth to race to the finish line, although it may feel like that sometimes. **We were placed on this Earth to make an impression.** We were placed here to share our talents and aspirations and give this world all we have to offer. Over time, if we continuously appreciate the small things and give it all we got, we will see that the end result approaches us in harmony. Success doesn't have a timeline—there are only suggestions. Each and every one of us deserves to create our own paths, create our own timelines, and enjoy every minute of peace in between. Society tends to force an image of "the perfect life" as being a race when in reality, it's an adventure and we create our own perfect lives. Allow yourself to live out your own path, not someone else's.

(Maybe) Deciding to Put Things on Hold or Transfer

Deciding which college to attend is not an easy thing to do. If you spend some time in your new home and then realize that it may not be the right place for you, *I'm here to tell you that's okay*. If you feel like you've picked the wrong school, you may feel like it's the end of the world right now. You may feel like it's impossible to make friends and that you are too far from home and that nothing seems to feel right at all. It is completely okay to transfer schools. Although your parents may be upset about that, it's an obstacle you (and they) will get over.

You may feel like entering college happened too fast and that you need some time to focus on yourself. Taking a semester off is not as serious as you think. If you keep up your motivation to get back into things, some time off is not going to affect the rest of your life. There are only a few months in the semester, and your mental health is more important than finishing school on time. Stress to your parents or guardians that you need some time to yourself and/or that you want to look into other colleges to attend.

This is only a minor bump in the road, and as they say, *this too shall pass.* Your newly chosen college may be a way better place for you. You cannot beat yourself up over not having known that right out of high school! Take some deep breaths, do some research on your new school, and present the issue to your guardians lightly. Even if they are angry in the beginning, they will soon realize that your happiness matters more than staying somewhere you don't feel comfortable.

I know people who have transferred schools and ended up in a place they couldn't have even dreamed about. They went from hating each and every day to never wanting to leave the place they ended up calling home. They made new friends almost immediately, loved their new roommate, and enjoyed everything their new professors had to say. Every college is different, and not every college can be a home for each and every person. While it's true that you need to stick things out for a little and know for sure that you're making the right decision to leave (it's possible things will get better for you), it is not the end of the world if you cannot fathom being at your current school for much longer. Switching schools may feel stressful, but focus on your happiness and know that there is a home for you out there. You will find it.

Some Freshman Advice

Get an early head start on your finances. This is a grown-up thing that doesn't come in short waves—on the contrary, you will soon realize how much each and every thing costs. If you are not lucky enough to have financial help going into college, you'll want to know some ways to get ahead in the financial game. College is expensive. Yes, I mean the academic costs, but it doesn't stop there.

Once you get to college, you will quickly learn that you'll have to spend money on a lot more than just tuition.

If you haven't yet sat down and learned about credit cards, I suggest you go to your bank and talk about getting your first one. A credit card will build your credit and give you some wiggle room to pay expensive things off over time instead of all at once. Having a credit card during college allowed me to work for things I wanted while also assisting me in paying for things I needed. But know that you need to be responsible about your finances and pay your credit card bill off on time. If you do not think you are ready to do that, then don't get a credit card.

You should also take advantage of small ways to make money. In college, I sold my old clothes and paid for all of my textbooks with the extra money, for example. Look into different jobs on campus and other ways you can save up some extra money. In a few years, you will have to worry about bills, rent, and extra payments. Be smart now and don't get yourself into debt while in college. You will save yourself a lot of trouble later.

Let's talk about textbooks. As you start your freshman year, you will be bombarded with a long list of necessary textbooks for every single one of your courses. The professors will most likely stress that you will not be able to pass the class without the material. I'm still not sure why professors believe in this when half of the time I never actually opened my textbooks and yet still passed with flying colors. Don't get me wrong—if you are in serious classes (such as most science or engineering classes), then you may actually need the book, or you might need it if your professor assigns homework or quizzes solely based on the readings. However, to save yourself a serious amount of cash, before you buy any textbooks, *do your research on each class.* Websites and various online resources may have information pertaining to the professor and how they teach the class. Also, if you check the syllabus, you may be able to determine if the assignments are based on the textbooks. **It is worth researching if you'll ever actually need these books, because believe me, they can add up.** If you decide that you do need the material, the most cost-effective way of going about this is looking for an *eBook* option assuming that you have easy access to a computer. If an eBook version is not available, your best bet is to buy the textbook used off of a textbook resale site or from an alumni who may be reselling them. Buying the book new is pretty much pointless and can cost a pretty penny. Also keep in mind that if you have access to a computer, you may be able to complete the assignments utilizing the resources you already have. Your online resources will become your best friends throughout your college career. They're mostly free and almost always will have the information you are looking for. Be smart about textbooks and make sure you are not spending money for no reason.

Your email is everything. Prior to applying to college, you may have never really checked your email. You may have not even had an email account. But once you arrive at college, checking your email is one of the most important things you can do. Your email will be your hub of information regarding events, school news, class cancelations, assignments, etc. There will be emails you do not want to skip reading. (Showing up for a class that was cancelled is a huge bummer.) Sometimes professors will also change the room that your class is supposed to be in—you will certainly want to know that information, too.

Checking your email can also be extremely beneficial in terms of campus events. Some campuses will provide free lunch one day or free activities on another day. Take advantage of this—after all, it is a part of what you are paying for. College campuses provide free food somewhere on campus almost every day, and your email will help you find these awesome benefits. Your email will also tell you about financial aid deadlines, employment opportunities, and other information you need to keep yourself up to date with. Bottom line: keep actively checking your email.

Take advantage of your resources. Your university is there to help you in any way they can. For example, they will have numerous scholarships that anyone can apply to. To apply, they will almost definitely ask for an essay, something that will seem like too much work on top of the other thousand assignments you need to complete. But here's the thing: applying is worth it, because it is free money you never have to pay back. These scholarships typically do not have many applicants, meaning that the competition is low and the possibility of you receiving the award is high. Some of these scholarships are awarded for leadership skills, cultural reasons, athletic experiences, etc., or are major-specific. Writing a short essay about yourself can result in a handful of cash.

Your campus will also host events in your residence halls that will allow you to meet more people. These events may seem overrated, but most of the time there is free food and you'll get to socialize. Free food in college is always something you should take advantage of. And always try to attend the events on campus! They are created for students to enjoy and most of the time they are actually really fun. **You are paying to be in college, so while you are there, make the most of every day and take advantage of your resources.**

Lastly, do not be afraid to ask if various establishments in the community (restaurants, shops, concert venues, etc.) offer a student discount. As a college student, you are able to receive student discounts for a lot of things, but chances are that businesses will not tell you this unless you ask. Some subscriptions are even half-price for students and some retail stores offer discounts for students. It's a good habit to ask before you pay—a lot of times, you will be surprised at the response. It never hurts to ask!

Keep your friends close and keep your professors closer. Having a close relationship with your professors will be more beneficial than you think. Making sure each one of them knows you by name will help you throughout your entire four years in college. You have to remember that your professors are ultimately in charge of your grades. While they are grading papers and tests, if they can put a face to a name, that will most definitely work in your favor. Although it will be the last thing you probably want to do, make it a point to go to their office hours even if it's just to talk about the class material for ten minutes. In their minds, it means a lot to them that you took the time to go. Ask them how their day went, pay attention to them during class, and always make it a point to say goodbye to them when leaving. If you didn't do so great on an exam or project, they are more likely to give you extra credit or grade your paper on the higher side.

All of that said, every professor is different, and some won't care at all that you pay attention to how their day is going. Still, it's worth a shot when it involves your grade. If it's a class you are not doing great in, make sure you are constantly asking your professor if there is anything you can do. Worrying about your grade says a lot to them. Keeping your professors close will also set you up for later in college when you may need a letter of recommendation or an internship opportunity. Your professors are part of your networking efforts, so respect them and make sure they know who you are.

Make room in your schedule for a useful-for-life class like economics. Chances are that during your freshman year, you will have some room for free electives. If your schedule allows for it, use these free electives for classes that are going to benefit you. Although it can be nice to choose classes that will give you an easy A, remember that you are paying to attend college. You are paying to gain knowledge that you will carry with you forever.

Taking an economics class was one of the smartest choices I made early on in college. It allowed me to learn different ways of managing finances and how the economy works and gave me business insights into certain things. If you have some extra time in your schedule, spend it on courses that are going to help you in the long run. Other good-for-life classes like this include cooking classes, health and nutrition classes, public speaking classes, etc. Do not forget that you are in college to learn. You have the ability to further your own knowledge in anything, so be smart when deciding what to learn about.

CHAPTER 3

The Holidays

I T'S YOUR FIRST WEEK BACK IN YOUR OLD stomping grounds
since you've learned what going to college actually entails. Your
parents are excited for you to return, and so are your weird
Uncle Jim, your Grandma Rose, and everyone else who just can't
wait to hear where the past few months have taken you. They have
been waiting for this day ever since you left. And I don't mean just
waiting to see you but waiting to ask the one question that has been
on their mind since you left: "What major have you decided on?"
Or even better: "So what have you decided to do with your life?"
Awesome, Aunt Pam! Great to see you, too.

Don't get me wrong—they'll be happy to see that you've survived
your first few months of independence. But if they're anything like
my family, all they want to know is what path you have inevitably
chosen. Can you blame them? They're excited to hear about what
their beloved gem has chosen to conquer. My one piece of advice
here is this: **Tell them you are going to be a doctor so that they**

never ask again, and when you graduate with a liberal arts degree, flee the country. Okay, maybe not flee the country, but worry about that when the time comes. The less information you give them, the less likely they are to feel that they have to keep asking.

I always struggled with what to tell my family. I always wanted to tell them what I had recently decided to go with because I was so excited about it, but in the end, I always realized that I should have kept things to myself until I was absolutely sure. Telling them about a new major every holiday led to confusion and exhausting explanations.

Through my experience, I found that other people—especially family members—are going to nudge their concerns into your life choices more than you will. You tell your Aunt Beth you've decided to be a teacher and that you have changed your major to education, and she stresses that the quality of life for teachers is going down the drain. You listen to her, and then you start to realize that you really like your criminal justice classes and you would love to be a detective. After you tell your Uncle Steve that, he tells you you can't start on that career path until you've been a traffic cop for at least 20 years. So for once in your life, you listen to Uncle Steve and decide that majoring in marketing will mean that you'll be 100% set up to make enough money to shut your family up even though you HATE your business classes.

The truth is that everyone is going to have an opinion—good and bad—on what you ultimately choose. For some reason, though, people only like to shine bad news on your delightful career paths. It is only when you listen to yourself and pick a major based on your desires that you will find peace. Be stern here and assure everyone that they *really cannot* change your mind. Remind them that you *will be great at anything you do* and you can't wait to pursue your career choice. As I said back in Chapter Two, your major

DOES NOT reflect completely on where your life will take you. So yes, Grandma, becoming a doctor is the only thing in the cards, and don't ask me again until after I've graduated from college.

Okay, so you're home and you've finally gotten past the semi-painful holiday dinner. You've assured your family that you are going to be a brain surgeon and it's the absolute best path for you to take. Now your friends from high school are all getting together. *Here we go...*

Luckily, not many of your high school friends are going to ask about your career path choices—mostly they just talk about themselves and you listen. You realize how much a few months away from each other can really change the dynamic. Saydee, we were only gone for a few months, and you date girls now? Justin, I just saw you four months ago. How have you already decided you are moving to France after you finish school?

Once again, in high school, we are shut into an environment with the same people for four years. We learn to tolerate those around us just because we are all in a boiling hellhole together for years and the only way to survive is to do it together. You may have loved the way Jessie braided her hair on the side all those years, so much so that you actually began doing it yourself...only to realize that your hair looks horrible in braids.

It's hard to understand the sense of conformity high school brings until you cut the umbilical cord and find what hairstyle (and everything else) looks best on you. In the beginning few months or even years that you return home to the friends you once dearly valued, you begin to notice that these friends whom you held so close to you are really nothing like you at all. **It's heartbreaking at first, but you need to remember that they shaped you into the lovely human being you are today.**

It's okay that during senior year, you and Julia spent every waking second together and now you struggle to converse about day-to-day things. It really is fine that once you and Jordan would have done anything for each other and now he's got a college girlfriend he can't go two minutes without talking about. Growing apart from people you used to be close with is more common than not, especially in terms of high school friends. After all, you were a whole different person during those four years—now that you have flourished into someone more like yourself, these people may want nothing to do with you. And if they seem like they're remaining glued together but you are becoming more left out, *the truth is that you are growing and they are not.*

If that's indeed what is happening, keep in mind that your high school friends are not going to take this different scenario lightly. They might treat the situation in an immature way and make you feel like it's your fault that you've grown away from them. **Never forget that growing into a new person is not something to apologize for. People either grow with you or grow away from you. This is something you'll deal with throughout your entire life.** Like I said earlier, high school is mostly about tolerating those around you, whereas in college, you can surround yourself with people who complement your personality. You need to cherish the times you've had with your high school buddies and remember that without them, you wouldn't be who you are. But at the same time, you need to accept that they are your past and that if they do not want to make it to the next level of your future, they shall stay in your past. This isn't to say that it's impossible to keep your friends from high school on your bridesmaids list or your lifelong buddies list, it's just that you need to be aware that you may want to stick with them or you may wind up growing in a different direction. **Most importantly, do not let them or anyone from your past stunt your incredibly beautiful growth as a human.**

CHAPTER 4

Your High School Relationship

D EPENDING ON WHERE YOU ARE IN YOUR LIFE right
now, reading this section might offend you, motivate
you, hurt you, or all do three. You may have not gotten
the chance to have a relationship at all yet. If that's the case, skip
this section and save yourself laughing over how horribly wrong it
could have gone if you did. Relationships can't be generalized,
and you cannot expect a life advice book (or really anyone) to tell
you how to feel. I can only suggest steps you can take if you feel like
you are clinging to a piece of floss that's pulling in direct opposition
to the person you thought you'd end up with forever.

Just as your high school friends are moving in opposite direc-
tions, so is the person you've been hanging on to for the past few
years and calling the love of your life. If you're anything like me, at
age 17 you were absolutely sure that you had found the person you
were going to be with forever despite what everyone else said. You

need to value those emotions and cherish the times the two of you shared, but *cherish that more as a growing experience than as memories*. Going into college, you have both agreed that your relationship is going to work no matter what. That it's the two of you against the world. But then reality hits, and you realize that the experiences you are going to endure over the next few years will have more to do with shaping you into the person you'll become than your high school relationship is going to have/could ever have.

Maintaining your relationship is hard. It is so f@ck*ng hard that you begin to lose yourself. Your significant other isn't answering your texts even though you know they got out of class six hours ago, and you're losing your sh*t. You lock yourself in your car and scream-cry for hours. You are absolutely sure at this point that you're falling off the deep end. I mean, can you blame yourself? For a long time, you've thought that finding a life partner was checked off the list and that no matter what happened, you would end up back together. You thought you knew what love was, what caring so much for another person felt like. It's my greatest joy to tell you that although those experiences were great, *there is an actually even better relationship in your future.*

You've read so many posts about this...soooo many. So many that you actually convince yourself that you've moved on. But trust me when I tell you that even when you think you've moved on, you really haven't. It will be hard for a little while longer. You will lose hope for a little while. But then, eventually, you'll start to find joy and happiness in other things, and before you know it, you barely even think about that person anymore. BOOM. Right before your eyes, Prince Charming/Queen Bee in their raw form comes to save you from this scary world. They've got you in their arms and the two of you are running off into the sunset before you even realize what is going on.

This isn't the person you've filled the void with for the past three years. This is a person who makes waking up fun, going to a wedding braggable, and going grocery shopping eventful. You look forward to doing small things together, like getting sushi or going to Walmart. Unlike the ex you so (eventually) gratefully let go of, this person you're now in a relationship with thinks you are out of this world, that you're an unexpected dream and an actual superhero. You had never really thought you would be with someone so fantastic until you find yourself already in the sandstorm of someone spectacular.

Mind you, this might not happen early on—you may need to experience different things with different people before you meet the one who can hold you forever. But here in Chapter 4, I'm telling you about your happy future so that you do not lose hope the way I did. I do not want you to let your past define the way you look at your future. What happened to you in the past should not alter the way you treat people moving forward.

I know that it's easy to let your past consume you, but I'm here to tell you that you are better than that. If you've been through a relationship rollercoaster by the time college rolls around, it's important for you to know that your former relationship is not the end of you. **You are not hard to love. You are not a bad person.** You are not going to be a crazy single cat lady/man your whole life.

You may feel like you have become incapable of feeling emotions. You are definitely convinced that love is nonexistent and that even if it does exist, you'll never know it. What has happened here is you have shut off your ability to open up to anyone. Even if you feel like the same you, underlying damage from your previous relationship is most likely preventing you from moving forward. This will only heal with time; you need to know that what you are feeling is completely normal. Although you cannot see it now, a day will come when you will actually emotionally feel like yourself again.

Whether you think that is a dramatic statement or not, I've been there. For those of you who feel like I'm reading your mind right now, take it from someone who walked around empty-hearted for too long: there is hope, there is real unconditional love, and you will absolutely find the person who offers you that love. When you do, you will feel like you never actually knew what love was before. You were convinced you knew what love felt like, but little did you know there was even stronger love out there, a more pure love that's worth holding onto forever.

So although that pain in your chest feels like it's a knife that will kill you, it is only an arrow that will make you stronger. You will go from holding onto someone who once thought they knew you to being embraced by someone who has come to know you now. Someone who will learn everything about you—*and I mean everything*—and will still accept you for all you are. Whether you are 21 or 45, once you find your person, everything that didn't make sense before will all come together. Everyone needs a different amount of time to heal their past wounds. You may feel one day that you healed, but no one has come along to sweep you off your feet. But they *will* come, and you will question why you spent so much time hurting over someone who clearly wasn't the one for you. Better things lie ahead.

Then again, some of you may find that you are quite happy on your own. You may find that spending time solo has made you feel more like yourself than anyone else ever could have ever made you feel. Some of us grow up with a freeing sense of independence, and that should not be altered by another person. Listen to your heart. If you find that you are better off non-partnered and your emotional needs are met through friendships, cherish that. There is no set of rules out there that insists you find someone to spend your life with, so keep this in mind as well.

The lesson to take from all of this is to just go through the motions—heal your own heartache in different ways and do what you absolutely love. Once you immerse yourself in activities you love doing and surround yourself with people you love being around, you will effortlessly come across someone who is lost in the same ways you were. It will feel like you've found a missing puzzle piece that was hidden just out of sight. You felt like it was so far away, but it really wasn't that far away at all. And when you do finally find that missing piece/person, the two of you will be unstoppable.

Finding your puzzle piece is almost like when you were younger and believed in Santa. Santa would never come when you were awake and looking for him—he would only come after you had gone off to sleep. Similarly, your person will not appear if you are constantly looking for them, so just do your thing and pay no mind. They will show up. Coming from someone who had no hope for love for a long time, I'm telling you that it's out there for you and you will eventually have the honor of knowing it. Be patient and focus on yourself. That's when someone will fall in love with everything you are about.

CHAPTER 5

The Love You Deserve

N O, THIS BOOK IS NOT ALL ABOUT RELATIONSHIPS, hoping for love, or getting over your ex. It's about getting through tough times in your life and hearing that you are not the only one thinking these thoughts. Thus, if you hate romance, I suggest you skip this chapter. I don't blame you if you do hate love—if you had told me a year ago that *I* would be writing about romance in any form, I would have laughed at you.

We go through phases in our lives that cause us to believe we don't deserve the epic love we see in movies. We convince ourselves that we will never find the kind of love fantasized about on social media or on TV. Personally, I found myself questioning if that type of love even existed. Just as I did in the previous chapter, I want to stress to you that *you will find that love.* You will find that person who makes every little thing in your life better. Sh*t, if *I* did, you will, too.

The only reason you feel half-complete is because there is

someone else out there who holds the other half of you. Although this book isn't meant to be a soppy love novel, I think it's important to remind you that yes, love does exist. Don't be cold to everything around you like I or others around me may have been. This concept might be hard to grasp right now, when you are constantly surrounded by crumbling relationships and "relationships" that can't even claim to *be* relationships.

A true relationship is being with someone you actually do not want to spend a moment without, someone who becomes your best friend. It's about finding the person who can complete your sentences or even your thoughts; the two of you might not even need to speak. College isn't always the best place to find this kind of love, so if you feel lost without any hope, remember that you have plenty of time to find your person.

The main takeaway here is that you *do* deserve someone who will barge in and shine light on your life. You *do* deserve a motivator, someone who makes you laugh constantly, someone you don't want to let go of. Enough of walking around empty-hearted and losing hope for years to come. I saw too much of this in college. Know that you are wonderful and that you will find someone who reminds you of that every single day.

If you feel like you *have* found that person, you should know that a few things may now seem odd but are in fact normal. Your closest friends will at times become more distant, and that's okay. The more time you spend with your significant other, the less time you will spend with the people you used to spend every second with. This happens fast, and it's almost out of your control.

If you're on the other side of that equation, you know it's difficult when your best friend gets into a relationship—you're probably feeling sidelined. But know that your friend hasn't stopped caring about you by any means. They cherish you just as much as they did before. The difference now is that their time is a lot harder to manage because more people are involved.

If you are entering into a new relationship or have been in one for some time, it's important to remember that a relationship should be two people each giving 100%. If the person you are with is your forever person, then your joint relationship should total 200%! Know your worth, and know that if you are being treated poorly, it's time to move on. Someone better is out there. Do not waste time on someone you constantly wish you were getting more from. Think about it this way: if you are spending time wishing you were getting more from someone, then you are preventing your Prince Charming/Queen Bee from finding you. The equation should not be 70% to 30%. It honestly shouldn't even be 50% and 50%. Each person should be giving 100%! You can both be complete and be just that much better when you are together.

Keep your head up even if a relationship you really cared about doesn't work out. Know that there is room in your heart for someone better. College is a time to focus on yourself, so if your significant other is getting in the way of that, kiss them goodbye. Your priority right now is to grow! If someone is preventing you from flourishing, that person and that relationship is not worth your time. Your person should be someone who helps you develop into the person you're becoming. College is about you and your progression, not someone else's. Of course, if they help you be the best version of yourself, then yes, stick around.

Also remind yourself that finding a significant other is not a "requirement" in life. If you feel that you would rather spend your life non-partnered, there is nothing wrong with that. Friends and family can easily fill the emotional needs in your life. My advice regarding romantic relationships is meant to give you some guidance if you *do* choose to be with someone. And please remember that it is imperative that you are happy with yourself before you even consider being with someone else. Do not rely on a partner to bring you happiness! Make sure you are happy within your own skin first.

CHAPTER 6

Sororities/Fraternities

THIS PART OF THE COLLEGE EXPERIENCE DIFFERS FROM person to person. When you get to college, you can either find a group of friends who are against the formality of Greek life or you can wait until the second semester to find your friends in Greek life. Whether or not you ever get roped into a sorority or fraternity, *it is super important to never lose sight of the important things.* In my college career, I joined Greek life late to add spice to my not-so-spicy sophomore year. As you read this section, please keep in mind that I came across many great people, found job connections that later led me to my lifelong friends at a different school, and became president of the whole damn sorority. Choosing to get involved in Greek life on campus can lead you to many different opportunities. I have absolutely no regrets about my life choice to join a sorority. *However...*

If you join Greek life, remember to keep your own values and beliefs close by your side. Many people subconsciously forget what they believe in and adopt the opinions and attitudes of their peers. You may find that your newfound group of people is super cool, but whatever you do, *stay true to yourself.* Do not let the pressure of your peers dictate what you do by any means. Sure, let's be real—we all know what joining Greek life means for the first couple of months. But if you get through all of that, do not let anyone change the way you are. Continue to say hi to people you always said hi to outside of Greek life. Be your sweet self to everyone you come across and do not let a new group of people get in the way of that. Stay well-rounded and always remember that although you now have sisters or brothers, this should not mean forgetting about everyone else who goes to your school.

Partying a bunch and building good relations with fellow Greeks can be extremely beneficial in regards to self-progression, and I highly suggest getting involved in any way you can once you are in college. You just need to remember that always being kind even if the people around you aren't will take you to higher places than any organization ever will. Never lose sight of your own personal morals and do not be afraid to stand up for yourself. Chances are some older members will not always treat you in a respectful manner. Remember, standing up for yourself can actually turn out in your favor! By establishing your own personal values, you will set an example for everyone around you. Be strong and never stop being yourself in any situation.

Getting involved within your fraternity or sorority can have many benefits. Your involvement can teach you the business side of things, organizational skills, time management skills, etc. But when your older brothers and sisters are encouraging you to get involved, you need to keep in mind that having a huge role in an organization is not an easy task. The bragging rights you'll get will only last a few weeks, and then you will be left with the actual duty of pulling your organization along. This inevitably comes with problems, responsibilities, and a good amount of stress. When I became president of my own sorority, I learned that I had taken on a full-time job I actually had to pay to do. Not only was I working for free and taking time out of my schedule for some words printed on my résumé, in a way, I lost sight of the fun part of being in a sorority. Parties became places where I constantly needed to deal with things going wrong, fundraising events became more stressful than enjoyable, and everything around me became a job.

So although it is great to be a leader at all times and to always be that person people look up to, you must consider the tasks that come with taking on this kind of leadership role before you commit to it. Consider the inherent long-term responsibilities rather than just the satisfaction of winning the election. This is not to say you can't handle it—by all means, you can. It is just a slight warning to know exactly what you are signing up for before you actually sign up.

Another aspect that needs to be considered before you go out and enter the world of Greek life is the attendant financial costs. This is something that is left out of the handbook, and it's something that almost no one will tell you the full truth about. When they tell you your dues per semester, they tell you the price you pay to just *be in* the organization. They do not include all of the extra costs: the t-shirts, getting a new addition to your branch, the outfits, the extra dues to pay for alcohol for your parties. All of these costs can easily add up to equal the base amount you pay to be a member in the organization. If your parents/guardians don't help you with your payments, be aware that on top of your monthly rent and expenses, you will be draining your pockets to keep up with the payments involved in Greek life. If you have a job, you will also have to take fewer shifts to make room for the demanding events your organization requires. Paying for all of that with less of a monthly income is not an easy thing to do. Make sure you have enough money saved before you commit to doing something this costly.

Other than the potential financial extremities, the occasional pressure to conform, and the stress that comes with having a leadership position if you choose to become part of Greek leadership, joining a sorority or fraternity can be a great way to make friends, get involved, and make your college experience better than ever. Like I said at the beginning of this chapter, everyone's story is different, and Greek life may or may not appeal to you. If you *do* join, stay true to yourself—both in Greek life and everyday life—and do not lose sight of other important aspects of your life. Remember the reason you are at college. Do not get lost in the sauce here! Keep your grades up and always put them before your organization's needs. Make time for other activities and people outside of your organization. Do not forget that Greek life is less important than a lot of people make it out to be.

CHAPTER 7

Spring Chicken

✳

ASSUMING YOUR COLLEGE IS IN A REGION WITH various seasons, by now the birds are chirping and day-longs are approaching. Spring is on the way! You've spent the last few cold winter months trying to avoid going to class at all costs, hiding your frat-kets in the best drawer available in the frat houses, studying for midterms, and praying it snows so your classes get cancelled. As the days get warmer and the months fly by, you can't help but to wonder how it is that your first year of college is almost over. While this may mean that your days of sharing an unethically small cubical room, dragging your laundry across campus, and having to admit you are a freshman to upperclassmen is almost over, *you need to slow down and appreciate your time here.* You'll hear me say this throughout this entire book because it's one of the most important values to keep close. Of course, with everything that's going on around you, it's easy to forget about needing to feel appreciative, so I am here to remind you every chance I get.

Everyone will tell you to slow down when you admit that you cannot wait to move into a real apartment or that you are extremely excited to be one year closer to graduation. *Listen to them.* Just as this past year flew by, the other three will go by even faster. Although you won't miss heating up your cup of ramen in your microwave under your bed, you *will* miss not having a damn thing to worry about besides doing decently well in school and having a kick-ass time. Freshman year may limit you to not having your car on campus, but it's the only time you can respectably use that as an excuse, so use it! Wallow in the semi-low expectations your freshman year blesses you with. Bask in the times you get to go out every single night of the week and can still pass all of your classes. Someday soon, you'll have to make adult decisions, like how you're going to pay your bills and whether you need to get work done and or you can go out. **I really can't stress this enough: be a freshman for as long as you can.**

Some aspects of your freshman year aren't necessarily going to follow you into your sophomore year, but you might not realize that yet. For example, you love eating in the dining hall and knowing pretty much every person who walks in (or you at least know who they are), but as the years progress, the number of people you are familiar with decreases. New faces will start to dominate the places you felt safe in. I'm not insinuating that this is a bad thing—meeting new people is great as well. Just appreciate the upperclassmen you will miss once they have graduated.

So while you're still in your freshman year, go out on the nights you know you shouldn't, stay up until your 8 a.m. class the next day, take care of yourself while doing so, and live each and every moment you have to the fullest. This is your time to make memories! This is your time to meet people you may be close to forever, people you will live to tell those crazy freshman stories with years down the line. **This is your time! Make the most of it.**

Your First Spring Break

It's almost time for your first college spring break. You've been imagining how this could play out since you were young; growing up, movies and shows helped build up your fantasies. Now the time has finally come to live them out. All of the friends you've made since you got to college are getting ready to drink their little hearts out on the beaches of Cabo or Punta Cana or wherever. If you are lucky enough to be able to financially swing that yourself this year, you have been counting down the days since you made your first payment towards your trip.

This section of the book is going to be short, because as they say, "What happens on spring break stays on spring break." A lot of us aren't lucky enough to go on spring break our freshman year. Whether it's for financial reasons or something else, know that you are not the only one who's not going and that you have three more years to make the trip. Early on in college, I went on small trips with a few friends for my spring break. I only did a huge spring break one year, and between me and you, one year was enough for me! Below are a few tips and tricks to get you through this week of catastrophic events if you are fortunate enough to go.

1. Hydrate

Most importantly, although it may not seem like the coolest thing to do during this week, **drink lots of water.** This small tip will make the difference from being like your friend Tammy, who blacked out at the pool party and didn't make it to the best night of the week, and your friend Liv, who got wasted at the pool party *and* made it to the club that night. While Tammy takes hours to wake up the next day and continues to throw up through the afternoon, both you and Liv will already be ordering mimosas at the pool...*and glasses of water, of course.* Water will be your saving grace! Even if you have to chug cups of water on the side while no one is watching, it will be worth it. Or even better, stick to vodka waters so you get the best of both worlds.

2. Sunscreen

You get to your destination, and everyone immediately takes advantage of the open bar of watered-down shots and sugary frozen drinks. You are all so damn excited to be there! The cheers of "It's spring break!!" distract everyone from the beamingly hot tropical sun. If you listen to anything I say in this section, *apply sunscreen as soon as you get there.* Not only will you save your skin from skin cancer and protect yourself from getting wrinkles, you will *save yourself from having an embarrassing night.* You will quickly learn that the people who remembered to put on sunscreen will be in way less pain than those who neglected it.

As the sun starts to set, everyone will look at each other in pure horror, realizing they completely forgot the power the sun has. (This is even before they get the chance to shower for the night ahead, and we all know that sunburn appears even worse after a shower.) After everyone goes off to shower and get ready for the night, those who are bright pink will soon regret their forgetfulness. Believe me, this advice all comes from my own mistakes. While you easily slip into the tight spring break dress you've been waiting to wear, your friends may have to result in baggy t-shirts or flowery sundresses.

3. Spring Break Drama

It's spring break—you have to expect that Lilly's boyfriend will be caught kissing Jena on the beach. The drama on spring break is inevitable, and the way you involve yourself can make or break your time. This doesn't mean you should neglect your friends when they need for a shoulder to cry on or someone to vent to. This simply means that you should be there for them and smile…and that's about it. The more you involve yourself with the craziness going on, the more you'll lose sight of why you went in the first place. You paid an arm and a foot to drink on the beach legally, come back golden-brown, and make memories that you'll hold with you forever. You didn't travel all this way to get roped into secrets, sides stories, and petty drama. **Look out for yourself and stay neutral towards everyone around you.** That's how you will have the best time.

4. Keep Your Distance From Locals

It's important that wherever you go, you appreciate the culture you have immersed yourself in. Learn their way of life and hold these lessons with you. However, **DO NOT BUY ANYTHING FROM A LOCAL ON THE STREET, ESPECIALLY ILLEGAL DRUGS.** I don't mean to sound like a worried mom here, but I've seen the danger of doing this and feel the need to stress that danger to you. There is a high possibility that locals around you will attempt to sell you anything, both legal and illegal. They know tourists have money, and they will try to take advantage of that. I am not referring to local shops and stores—I'm talking about Benny on the sidewalk offering you fruit or cocaine. Although you may be dying for an extra boost to get you through the day, drink an energy drink or take a little nap. *Do not buy cocaine from Benny.* Locals will also jump on any chance they get to scam the tourists out the wazoo. That "Coach bag" Benny is selling for $100? It is not a good deal. *Do not buy anything from Benny.*

5. Stick Together

You are independent, and your love for traveling goes beyond blacking out on the beach and going to the same bars every night. You want to see what this place is all about. **Although you feel the urge to stray from the group and appreciate your surroundings, you need to resort to the old buddy system you learned about in Pre-K.** The world can be a scary place, and when you leave your trusted terrain, things can get more scary. When your parents/ guardians stress this before your plane takes off, *keep that thought with you.* Even if Mary complains when you drag her into stores, keep her close. Be smart and always travel in twos *at least.* This could be an excuse to get Mike/Michaela to stray from the group with you and look at the murals around the corner. Tell them that you were told to travel using the buddy system and use it as an excuse to spend some time with them.

If you follow these tips and tricks, your spring break will be a time you'll hold close to you for the rest of your life. And don't be afraid to meet other college students who are not part of your group—you may create everlasting friendships. Take advantage of those buy-one-get-one margs and stay up all hours of the night. Spring break is a time to forget your school worries, let go of reality, and bask in the sunshine. Take my advice and go get 'em, tiger!

CHAPTER 8

The Final Days

I T'S FINALS SEASON. YOU'RE BREAKING OUT, GAINING WEIGHT, and losing sleep. You are torn between the last nights of going out with your friends and getting an A on your acting final. There's no good option here: it's the last few nights of your freshman year, but you also need at least a B on your non-credit math final to pass the course. You are at the finish line. Don't give up! Do both. **Get up early even if you are still drunk from the night before and study for your exams so that you can live out your final nights.** Study your absolute hardest and truly appreciate the final nights you'll be with your friends, because once again, you will never get this time back.

Everyone around you will tell you to stay in and study ... which you should do, but I am saying you can do both. Depending on what school you go to, other students may actually be staying in during the week of finals. If they are, take advantage of the time you have to cram as much information in as you can. If people are nagging you to come out, take my advice and spend your time wisely. By this point, you know you are capable of doing both: you can study for a good amount of time during the day *and* spend a few hours out with your friends. Just be mindful of how late you stay out and how many shots you swallow—after all, it *is* finals week. Wake up early, drink a full glass of water, have a coffee, and get after it. **Your finals are incredibly important to your final grade. Do not take them lightly.** Only you will know if you can swing going out a night or two during finals. Listen to yourself, know what you can handle, and enjoy these last few days of being a freshman!

And although you'll need to move out of your dorm, pass your tests, and arrange a summer job, *try your hardest to live in the moment.*

PART TWO
SOPHOMORE SAGA

CHAPTER 9

Sophomore Scaries

IF IT WERE THE 90S, BELLS WOULD BE ringing, because class is back in session. The summer flew by faster than you could have ever imagined. You are back...and it feels like you never left. Only you did, and you're now a sophomore! It isn't long before you realize how much has changed in a few short months. If you ended up joining a sorority your freshman year, you are back with all of your Greek life friends. If you avoided that, you quickly realize the attention you got as a freshman has sort of fizzled out. The frat guys/older girls who were dying to know your name are more now interested in the incoming freshmen, and you start to feel less included. *Do not let this get the best of you.* Take getting less amount of attention from the older students as a blessing. Who wants to be in the spotlight for more than a year, anyway? Enjoy your newfound option of choosing exactly how you want to spend your time. Want to pick up a new hobby, start working out, or surround yourself with a different group of people? *Do it.*

Even more so than when you first got to school, sophomore year is the year for recreating yourself. Think about it: you entered college like a baby deer exiting the womb, and you were so unfamiliar with your surroundings that you were doing anything you could to stay afloat. Now, instead of worrying if you're wearing the right attire to the fitness center or stressing about finding where the hell they put the French fries in the dining hall, you are worrying only about yourself and who you may become.

This is an influential time for you, and you should focus on pursuing your true passions while also getting involved on campus as much as you can. Let's face it—if you are anything like me, you didn't do much during your freshman year to build your résumé. (Unless the title of beer pong champion is an acceptable point, of course.) So take this time to find clubs you enjoy, part-time jobs you don't hate, and people who will assist you in your adventure to the top.

This doesn't mean you should feel pressure to set yourself up to work for a leading company just yet, *although it wouldn't be bad if you did.* It just means you should be more aware of making the most of your time at college. Even though looking back on incredible memories is a must, you owe it to yourself and everyone around you to utilize your resources. **Socialize, create opportunities for yourself, and grow into becoming more of the beautiful, powerful human being you are.** Do things you are not sure you will enjoy. Jump into the unknown and just try a little bit of everything. Sophomore year is the perfect time for experimenting with different things, because at this point, you'll have plenty of time to drop the things you *don't* enjoy.

During my sophomore year, I started working for a huge company as an entry-level, part-time student. I came across the opportunity from someone I had just been friendly to, and that job ended up shaping my future both socially and professionally. You won't know if something is for you or not until you give it a try. This may mean applying to work at your campus recreational center to meet someone there in event management. Or you might start hanging out with your biology partner who has connections in the health field. It's all part of the wonderful path that lies ahead of you.

The best piece of advice I can pass on to you in your sophomore year (and beyond) is to **always involve yourself as much as you possibly can, because in the end, the people you meet will lead you to future opportunities more than your degree itself will.**

But enough with all this professional talk! You are definitely still going to be attending parties and waking up with morning hangovers. The difference now is that when you go to those parties, you will be able to clearly pick out the freshmen and you'll think to yourself, *Gosh, I hope I didn't look like that!* Don't worry—you totally did look like that, and yes, everyone saw. Let those freshmen live out their glory days. Sip your bottle of wine while they chug the jungle juice you couldn't get enough of last year. They are going to talk to you while you are waiting in line for the bathroom. Be kind and remember the times you just wanted to make friends in the new place you now call home. It's more difficult for freshmen to pick out who's older than them, and in their defense, it's their time to make all the friends they can, just as it was your time to befriend people a year ago.

Sophomore year is a year to cherish, because during your sophomore year, you are a veteran without being an old fart. You know your way around campus and you have learned the do's and don'ts, but you still know how to have a kick-ass time. You know a bunch of people and you feel like this may be your best college year yet. *Which it very well might be.* Stand your ground as a sophisticated sophomore but also stay humble and always be helpful to those around you. In the end, it is important to remember that no one can ever say anything bad about you if you are always kind to everyone. You may sense people around you getting rather territorial because they feel like it's their grounds now, but *stay neutral and be kind to all.*

Your Major

Back to the boring sh*t: your major. If you are lucky, you have already chosen a major you love and you have high hopes that you'll graduate and happily follow a related career path. But again, I can't stress this enough, *it's okay if you do not know what your major is going to be yet.* People around you may already be talking about internships, student teaching, etc., but not knowing is not a big deal. You may be pursuing a major that you picked under pressure and you've realized you hate. You still have time to figure yourself out. Chances are, you can pick a whole new major and still graduate on time. It may be hard to keep that in mind with all of society's bulls*@t talk in the background, but do not stress over figuring out what you want to do for the rest of your life. **Your degree does not define you.** My freshman year, I came into school with a biology focus, then changed to marketing, then to undecided, then to education, then decided to just graduate with a communication studies degree, and then ended up not wanting to do any of it. If you involve yourself, meet as many people as you can, and find different passions along the way, *your path will almost choose you.*

If it helps, read articles about how other people chose their major. There could be an aspect of your passions you are forgetting about. Read stories about how people who graduated with a journalism degree went on to work in the business field. Explore your different career options for each major. Most importantly, *do not ever feel discouraged.* During your sophomore year, you will still have a ton of time to figure things out, even if it doesn't feel like you do. Do your research and keep an open mind. Once again, you will always end up where you are supposed to be.

Getting Comfortable with Yourself

Spend time by yourself. Wake up early some days and drink coffee sitting on a bench in the middle of nowhere. Reflect on how far you have come and focus on the times that made you most happy. Realize that if you don't give your poor self a moment to think about what's going on around you, you won't be able to choose where you want your path to lead you. Times like these are extremely important for self-growth and progression. **Although it's hard to take a break from the events going on around you, find the time to pause whatever it is you have going on and focus on your own mind.** Your own thoughts are the only voice that will lead you in the right direction. You can do research to help direct your thoughts, but in the end, you are the driver of your own car. Suggestions from people on other walks of life can be helpful at times, but you ultimately need to focus on what's important to *you*. Write down what you're thinking, highlight the most important parts, and reread your thoughts every now and then. Organizing your life goals will be extremely beneficial to choosing a path.

I've never been one for meditating, but I do know that having a good mental relationship with your own mind can bring you to places you never thought you could/would go. If that means drinking coffee on a bench thinking about the boy/girl who caught your eye four days ago, then think about them. What matters most is creating a relationship with your own powerful mind. **Self-reflection can be your most powerful tool and one you can utilize throughout your whole life, so it's important to get familiar with this concept early on.** If you have the power to self-reflect, self-analyze, and hang out with your own mind, you are on the right track to doing big and beautiful things.

Friends are cool, but how you feel when you are around just yourself says a lot about your character. You have the power to shape yourself into literally whoever you want to be. You can alter your own thinking and change your opinions on certain things. Appreciate the power you have when it comes to thinking, because how you think will shape your actions on a daily basis. If you are constantly beating yourself up over something, that will show up in other aspects of your life. You need to take control of your own mind and let it know that you are in charge. Work on this! Thinking is more powerful than you'll ever realize…until, that is, you start to see a difference in how you live your life.

CHAPTER 10

Mental Struggles and Overcoming Them

ALTHOUGH I HAVE NEVER PERSONALLY BEEN A VICTIM of severe depression or mental health issues, I am well aware that they exist. I am here not to give advice on how to fight them, but I would like to share ways you can cope with these issues. College is an extremely tough time and not a lot of people acknowledge that. College isn't only academically difficult, it's difficult in every way possible. People like to sugarcoat how hard it is to be a young adult juggling a thousand things at once. I know from personal experience that college is not easy by any means.

Constantly fighting a mental health problem can feel impossible and make you feel defeated. But I promise you: you got this. You are continuously taking hits, whether it's not getting the internship you spent two whole hours applying for, getting denied by someone you worked up the courage to talk to, waiting in line for food for an hour only to then realize you no longer have time to eat, or somehow all three in the same day. **College puts you to the test every single day, and sometimes it all gets to be too much.** It is normal to feel this way when you are faced with a thousand obstacles on a daily basis. You are not being too hard on yourself—it is okay to feel like less of a rockstar some days. The truth is, we couldn't become as great as we do become without hitting some bumps in the road. That's how I want you to look at things from now on. I want you to know that if we never felt completely defeated, we wouldn't appreciate the times when we feel sky-high.

Mental health varies for every individual. What you feel may not be the same as what the person next to you feels, but I promise, we all deal with our own demons. We are all faced with difficulties every single day. This is why formulating the language we use with others is so incredibly important. You never know when someone is in the middle of a full-blown war zone of a mental battle. Be kind to all; be there for your friends who reach out to you and reach out to them if they seem distant. Mental health is a serious matter, and you can make or break someone without even knowing it. We are all here to support each other. Be the person you may need to lean on someday. In case *you* need someone to lean on, **I want to talk about some important ways to give yourself the lifejacket you need at times.**

1. A Bad Day is NOT a Bad Life

You have had a semi-bad week thus far. You wake up and your Keurig takes a sh*t. You finally get a cup of coffee out of it, but you drop it as soon as you walk out the door. You are running late, and when you finally get to class, you realize you have an exam that day. You botch the exam but find the courage to get over that ... when you realize you have an event tonight for a club you really care about. So you organize *that*, but you completely forget you told Jen/Josh you would hang out with them. You clear that up and run home to shower before getting lunch with Jen/Josh ... and you forget to bring a towel. You run naked across your apartment and almost make it to your room, but of course then the door opens and it's obvious that your roommate decided to have her study group over that day. F*ck!! This whole day has been so hectic you completely neglected to call your sister for her birthday. It's been a hard week, and it's only Tuesday.

You have surpassed your sense of rage; all you want to do now is break down and cry. Believe me, I have been there numerous times. I know that sometimes a bad day can feel like your life is absolutely crumbling apart. **But as hard as it is, you need to remember that a bad day is not a bad life.** A bad *week* is also not a bad life; neither is a bad month or a bad year. Your life is so huge that your days, months, and years are only super small segments of the incredible life you will live. So although sometimes it feels like you can't win for sh*t, you cannot let that defeat you. Stand tall during these times. Look your roommate's study group right in the faces and say, "Well, sh*t, this is my naked hour, and you are all interrupting." Cry for 20 minutes, scream into your pillow, and remember that believe it or not, these are the times that will make you stronger. **In the end, defeat is only encouragement—unless you let it consume you. You have the choice.**

2. You are NOT Alone

From my studies—both academic and anecdotal—I have learned that depression is a beast that makes you feel like you are the only person in the world. You feel like no one can understand what's going on in your head. You do not even want to attempt to explain things; you would rather just cuddle up in your bed and shut down. But instead of letting the feeling of being alone take over your thoughts, focus on the fact that you have yourself. Give yourself a mental hug and think of the qualities about yourself that you haven't seen in anyone else. You have the power to shine light on yourself!

When I say you are not alone, I mean that you are never alone because you have yourself. **You are your own person to lean on, to grow from, and to thrive from.** Besides the fact that you always have yourself to depend on, you have resources at your disposal to get you through the toughest times: you have professors who care about you, family members who think about you constantly, and peers who are concerned about you. And also know that you're not alone in the way you feel—thousands of other people feel the exact same way you do.

In moments of struggle, you may feel like knowing there are other people who are feeling the same way isn't enough. You may feel like you were just knocked off of a ten-story building and the last person you want to turn to is your own damn self. But instead of feeling like that, embrace your mind and the thoughts it's creating. Analyze the deepest, darkest struggles you may be facing and then look yourself square in the eyes and say "I am a f*ck#ng champion!" Think of the last thing you did that made you smile. Not what someone *else* did to make you smile, but something *you* did while you were alone that made you crack a smile.

As I've said before, this world can be a scary place, even more so while you're in college. The only way to power through it is to be your own rock. Have a relationship with yourself that you know you won't have with anyone else. You owe that to yourself! Become familiar with your weaknesses and your strength to overcome those. Write it all down if you have to. Do whatever you have to do to convince yourself that you are your own best friend, your own motivator, and your own personal best asset for society. **When I say** that you are not alone, this means that you will NEVER be alone if you find yourself. Work on it every damn day. **Create the person inside your head whom you want to be at your side throughout this journey we call life.** A close relationship with yourself will slay your inner demons. Always.

3. Just Keep Swimming

I know it seems hard to swim right now because you feel like you are already being dragged away in a riptide. Doggy-paddle your way out of this rut and *just keep going*! There will be obstacles, sea glass, tides—you name it—but you need to power through. Throughout your college career, you will find that at times you'll get tired of swimming, that you just want to stop altogether. It is vital that you get through these times despite what you may be feeling.

I'll never forget the time I stopped swimming. I curled up in a ball and let everything around me flood my ability to move past it. I closed my eyes for a solid 30 minutes, waiting for the tide to take me away. It's almost like when you are little and playing in the ocean, constantly getting beaten down by the tidal waves that don't stop coming. Your guardian comes running in fear that you won't get out alive. But when life makes you want to stop swimming, the only person coming to your rescue is *you*. You are your own savior. You feel like you may not be able to surface from the hardships around you, *but you must come to your own rescue.*

Through the assignments, the deadlines, the pressure of being yourself, *swim*. Swim elegantly, with purpose and dedication. Imagine you are in the middle of the beautiful waters of Hawaii. You *do* want to get to the other side because that's where the food is, and you know that no matter what comes across your path, you must keep moving forward. Swim, little fishy! Let the water help you follow your path. Swim in the direction you want to swim, look those obstacles right in the face, and overcome them so that you can get to where you need to be.

4. Life is About the Dance

I've mentioned this previously, but it's worth saying a thousand times: appreciate where you are. You are so caught up with trying to succeed, have fun, and take care of yourself all at once! Do not get lost in all of this (although some of it may be out of your hands). You spend so much time trying to stay afloat and get to your destination that you forget to appreciate every waking moment along the way.

When you are having a bad day, do not wish you could skip ahead to the next day—instead, simply live in the moment, even if it doesn't feel like the best one. Appreciate your hardships and wallow in your own pity for a little while. As Alan Watts says, if we continue to wish for the next step, we will eventually get there … only to realize we forgot to appreciate the current moment. For example, we go to elementary school just to reach middle school; after that, we go to middle school just to get to high school. We then go off to college to get a profession, but that's not enough, either. We get the promotion we have been working towards and we have finally reached what we have been preparing for for our entire lives … only to look back and realize we forgot to take the time to dance.

Dance in the present moment! Embrace the days you wish were different. Take time to reflect on how far you have come. Live each and every moment to the fullest. **Life is about so much more than just making it to the next step.** Life is about the now, the past, and what's to come.

Although this thought stuck with me throughout college, I admittedly often lost sight of it. Learn from my lesson! Take a pause on your thoughts and actions. Be in the current moment as often as you possibly can. Take a pause in the middle of a frat party or in the library during finals. Slow down and appreciate each and every moment. Look around you more often. Take pictures of the beautiful life happening around you. Appreciate the people you surround yourself with. **This isn't just college—this is every waking moment before and after it.**

CHAPTER 11

Social Media Habits

A T THIS POINT, THE INTERNET AND SOCIAL MEDIA are things we have all grown up with. We have grown up knowing what it is like to have everything we could possibly want right at our fingertips—we can access images, words, information, and social lives with the touch of a few buttons. It's liberating and empowering and a great resource at times. Social media is a powerful tool that we should always use to our advantage! It offers us opportunities to get noticed, showcase our talents, and keep in touch with people we may not see every day. We have the ability to learn new things, research topics we are interested in, and learn a whole new hobby from a how-to video. Do not take this chapter as a bash on technological advances.

But! As beautiful as all of this is, social media can be our biggest demon. Being the young adult you are, you need to know the severity of what you have access to. As you've heard numerous times, what you put on social media and the internet is never truly erased.

These people are not lying to you. You leave a digital footprint in *every single thing* you do online. With the freedom we all have, I want you to remember to always be conscious of how you are utilizing social media and all things internet. You need to remember that what you put online will be with you forever in some form or another. Do yourself a favor early on and be smart about what exactly you are putting out there! There are numerous reasons for this.

Safety first

Your #1 priority is your safety, of course. Be smart about adding your location to your social media activity, because you never know exactly who is looking at it. You need to keep in mind that although your friends are enjoying seeing your posts in specific locations, complete strangers are also enjoying those posts. This is not to scare you—this is to stress how dangerous it is to add your location on social media. Be mindful of everything you are putting out into the world, both for your safety and your reputation.

Your future job(s)

You also need to keep in mind that employers are utilizing social media as an opportunity to see who you truly are. Believe it or not, online profiles have become a deciding factor in the hiring process! So before you post those pictures of your favorite frat party, make sure you look like a presentable potential employee. Be aware of how you are representing yourself to those around you. Respect yourself and how you make yourself visible on a massively viewed platform. This can be quite difficult considering that the social media influencers we look up to do at times post graphic material. Do not follow in their footsteps! You are trying to nudge yourself into the professional world—posting risky pictures is not going to get you a job with a huge corporation.

IRL is important

Another aspect of technology worth discussing is how much you are active in your real life vs. how often you are active on social media. Although social media and online activities may often spark your interest, you must not forget that you should be partaking in real life as well. It's awesome to record amazing experiences so that you can look back on them, yes, but there are times you should put your phone or camera down and embrace the now. Live in the moment! Do not let your phone take that away from you. Far too many times, I've been at a concert and having the best time ... and I looked over to see a close friend watching the entire show through their phone screen. Your followers are not at the concert, *you* are. You want to spend time embracing the current moment. Limit your time on social media if you can.

It is understandable that you want to be involved online as much as you can. I am just here to warn you about the potential dangers of putting yourself online, plus I want you to live each and every moment to the fullest and never let technology get in the way. Spend time with those around you and take in this beautiful world with your own eyes! Limit technology as much as you can, because again, you will not get those times back.

CHAPTER 12

Friends with Benefits

A T SOME POINT IN COLLEGE, WE ALL LEARN about being in a relationship without having any of the "real stuff." It's confusing as hell and can be dramatic at times, but it's also pretty fun. You may meet someone at college whom you feel could be your best friend but *things get sticky and you end up being just slightly more than that.* It's unexpected and actually ends up making more of an impression on you than you would like to admit. This is someone you get super close with in every way other than the *feelings* aspect. Which is only semi-true, because although neither of you will ever admit it, you only spent that time together because there was some kind of feeling between you. There is no doubt that you care for each other in some way.

Then again, if you never end up coming across a friends-with-benefits scenario, you didn't miss out. But if you do wind up with a friend with benefits, I'm here to talk about the things you are both scared to say. You only keep each other around because you are both exploring new things and in the process find an unexpected attachment towards one another. You are comfortable enough to treat each other like a best friend while also expressing a desire to try things out. You both think the other is a super great catch—you wouldn't be doing this if you didn't think that. **But either it's not the right time or it's just not that deep, and that's what keeps the line from being crossed.**

You will most likely accidentally hurt one another in some way eventually, whether that happens when someone gets too attached or it happens because guidelines are not set out from the beginning. Signing up for a friends-with-benefits deal is signing up for slight emotional pain whether you like to admit it or not. It's not heartbreak—that is, if you're lucky—but it's close. When a FWB betrays you, you feel the hurt of a friendship and a significant other all at once. But because you've agreed that there are *no strings attached,* you try to hide your emotions. You are not fooling anyone, and neither are they. Of course, relationships cannot be generalized, so your particular situation might be different.

None of the above are reasons to avoid this type of relationship—in fact, they are meant to encourage you to embrace a FWB situation. Learn all you can from this dynamic! While it may feel like you are wasting your time, you will learn a lot in this relationship, namely the value of trust, the fact that people can betray you and that things aren't always as they seem. Most importantly, you'll learn that you deserve more than just "someone to pass time with." This is a relationship that will ultimately benefit you in more ways than you may realize at the time. If you are lucky, your FWB is a person you won't ever forget but will just grow past. **You'll realize that your time and energy are valuable.** And that they should be spent on someone who appreciates you and reciprocates your efforts *and vice versa.*

Here's where your story will probably differ from the next person's. I know people who ended up marrying their FWB, and I also know people who left their FWB in the past. Either way, it's best to enter the situation with some advice.

1. It is Never Too Early to Establish Boundaries

Things will never go well if you ask your FWB the dreaded question, which is "What are we?" They will panic ... or in some instances, they will ask you the same question, and *you* will most definitely panic. It's something that no one ever likes to think about, especially within the context of *"no strings attached."* Most of the time, the other person will freeze up and accuse you of asking that question too early. However, if you are indeed asking, it really is not too early at all—you can't blame yourself for wanting to know what the F is going on. You guys have probably been hanging out for some time now, and you just want to know if things are going anywhere or not. **This seems like a simple concept, but believe it or not, it is always blown out of proportion.** But stand your ground and ask your question. If they can't admit that all they want is you on the weekends, kick them to the curb. Or maybe they want your heart, in which case you might have a different answer.

2. Protect Yourself

Talking about protection is a conversation that can be totally awkward, but I'm here to tell you that it's a conversation well worth having. This is true throughout all of college and with everyone, not only the person you are consistently with. Protecting yourself in college will save you from some serious potential future issues.

Before entering college, using protection isn't talked about enough. There are diseases and STDs that our health teachers never even warned us about, and some of them can potentially stay with you for the rest of your life. Although we all like to think we are *not* prone to getting any of these scary diseases, the fact is that we are all at risk. I watched my friends in school sleep with one person and come home with something they were never able to treat or get rid of. It's real! Do not be afraid to protect yourself.

Considering that a friend with benefits situation usually includes no type of commitment, know that you are not safe with them, either. Be strong and know that it is seriously vital that you *always* protect yourself. STDs and STIs are real, and you are no different from the other thousands of college students worldwide who are affected by this. Someone just saying they're "clean" does not mean anything. This goes for everyone around you, not just your FWB.

3. Boundaries WILL be Blurred

So you finally get an answer out of them: they want you around, but they are not looking for anything serious right now. Fine. You accept that and you both continue with the relationship you have. Then one night you happen to end up at the same party. (If you go to a small school, this is a given; otherwise, it's a surprise.) One of you starts to pay attention to someone else at the party, because after all, no strings attached, right? Well, let me tell you something—that's not going to fly. Someone will get mad, sad, drunk, and/or verbal. The night will eventually result in some type of chaos. **So if you are reading this, spare your FWB unsaid feelings and flirt with Bryan/Brittney in the other room, out of their sight.** Your FWB won't admit that's why they are sad/mad ... or maybe they will. Either way, it's going to be a long night, so *buckle up.*

4. Don't Lose Hope

I don't want you to go into this relationship thinking it's immediately going to be flushed down the toilet, but I do want you to be aware of what comes with FWB scenarios the majority of the time. The best lessons I've learned were the ones I learned as a result of diving into the unknown. I didn't know if anything was going to come of it or if everything was. I can't know how your relationship will go, although I *can* tell you that *yes, it is a relationship*. It's up to the two of you to write your own stories. If you really care for the person and you don't want to let them go, don't give up! Just because you got off to a rocky start doesn't mean it won't end up working out in your favor. College is a stressful time for all, and sometimes adding on a committed relationship can just be too much.

The main takeaway from this chapter is to always communicate with the person you are spending time with. Even if they make that hard at times, always tell them how you are feeling. If you *don't* tell them, they will never know how you actually feel. Everything is better when it's all out on the table. You might learn that trotting around without a title makes you both uneasy because you actually want to be exclusive. Or you might like having a friend you care about being consistently around without any complications. A FWB is almost like a trial period at times. You either learn that you don't care enough to tie them down or that you can't stand the fact that they are going out without you.

At the end of the day, know your own value and worth. Do not spend so much time on Romeo or Juliet that you miss another opportunity who might be standing right in front of you. Enjoy the times when the two of you have pointless little arguments and never get ahead of yourself. Read the situation with an open mind … but also never forget this advice.

CHAPTER 13

Independence

YOU *SORT OF GRASPED THIS DURING YOUR FIRST* year of college: most universities cushion the freshman experience. When you first got to school, you may have had a roommate, so you never actually had to go places alone unless you wanted to. You may have had mostly freshmen in your classes, so if you messed something up, you were all in it together. Your dining hall experience might have also been freshmen-only, along with your dorm buildings and fitness centers. But as you go through your sophomore year, that separation is no longer there—you are *thrown to the wolves.*

It can sometimes be scary to feel like you're a tadpole in a pond full of frogs, but as long as you stand tall, you will make it through. Embrace the newfound options you have now! Empower yourself with the ability to choose exactly how you wish to spend every waking moment. Whoever may have helped you up to this point has most likely left things up to you. Unless you are one of the lucky ones who still calls Mom to help you food-shop, *it's each to their own now*. Your training wheels are either off or close to being off, and it's time to take advantage of your freedom.

The freedom to make choices is one of the most powerful aspects of being human, so make strong, healthy choices and create your own definition of independence. Do not let the upperclassmen intimidate you! Keep in mind that none of them know what the hell they're doing, either, *even if they act like they do*. It may be hard, but pay no mind to those who look down on people younger than them—they are only doing that because of their own insecurities. If you keep that thought with you through college, you'll be just fine.

With independence comes making your own choices. One of those choices might be studying abroad. Studying abroad can be the best experience of your life, but it does come with a high cost if your university doesn't offer affordable options. Still, it never hurts to look into study abroad programs and ask your advisors what your options are. If you decide that you and your family have the financial means, do it! Do not be afraid to "miss out" on your friends and your college life. I promise you, they will be doing the same things when you get back—you will not miss out on anything.

Exploring a different country while also pursuing your degree is not an option that everyone has. If you do have that option, take advantage of it! Living abroad will also make you more appealing to future employers, and you will make memories that you will hold with you forever. Although it may feel like you are going to be missing out on what's going on, you are doing the exact opposite, because you will have the adventure of your life and will learn many, many more life lessons than you could have learned if you had stayed at your home college all four years. Explore your abilities and take advantage of opportunity!

One of my own personal regrets about college is that I never made the jump to study abroad. I was too focused on the present day to prepare for a trip that long. If you feel like a whole semester is too long to be away, explore a winter semester or a summer option. Some immersion language schools in foreign countries also offer college credits, and you can typically attend those schools anywhere from a few weeks to several months.

Traveling can do a lot more for you than you think! You'll most likely be in easy elective classes abroad that will allow you to focus your learning on the place around you. You'll get a feel for cultural values and differences. If you're in a non-English-speaking part of the world, you'll gain at least some conversational ability in a foreign language; if you're already majoring in a language and do your study abroad during your junior or even senior year, you may be fluent by the time you come back home. (Being multilingual is not only an amazing life skill, you'll be eligible for a wider array of jobs.) You will also get to see how the economy operates in a different part of the world. Studying abroad offers many, many benefits. I suggest you do some research and consider it!

CHAPTER 14

Finding Your Style

✳

THROUGHOUT YOUR YEARS IN COLLEGE, YOU WILL ADOPT many different styles, just as you did in high school. Call these "phases" if you wish. You may have started out wearing skirts or boardshorts and ended the same year wearing the opposite. You started out dying to have those bright white sneakers everyone else had…just to finally get them and realize you would rather wear garbage bags on your feet. It's completely normal to go from being a goth to a skater boy/girl and come back around to liking preppy clothes. As I was going through each phase of mine, I wish I had had more confidence in my own style. Instead, I liked how other girls all started to wear the same thing at once and thought it looked cute, so I also bought that same bear coat at a boutique for $75. It's easy to conform to what everyone around you is wearing, but in a sense, now I wish I had paid more attention to myself and less to everyone else. In my last few years, I grew to like baggier clothes when everyone else was stuffing themselves into sausage casings. Baggy clothes made me feel smaller, and I liked that, but at times I looked around me and found that I kind of stood out. **Whether it feels like it or not, it's a good thing to stand out.** Focus on your own desires in clothing and accessories! Wear things that make you feel true to yourself. And if that means buying what everyone else does, that's fine, too.

Once you think you've found your forever style, all you want to do is spend *all* of your savings on related clothing so that you can really wallow in the vibe you've grown to love. You want to go on a shopping spree at Zumiez because you think you'll be a skater chick/boy forever. As hard as it is to not do this, *don't*. You will thank yourself in a few months when you find a new favorite store with a new favorite style. Having a style is more about accessories and how you present yourself than it is about individual pieces of clothing. Although it seems like planets away, in a few years when you are out of college and looking for jobs, you won't be able to wear your Vans and your skater tee to an interview. Buy a few things to get the taste out of your mouth and worry about your style via other ways.

A huge way I blew a lot of my saved-up money was thinking I had grown into my final stage or style. I spent a ton of money on these clothes and shoes only to realize it wasn't my final style at all. College is a time for saving money, and spending your savings on clothes and shoes that you swear you'll never grow out of is unethical and you will regret it. It's only a matter of time before you'll have to shop for suits and dress pants, and unfortunately, those are a lot more expensive than your Zumiez wardrobe.

CHAPTER 15

Sexuality

MM, COLLEGE! THE SWEET SMELL OF FREEDOM AND
expression. You are finally away from your family, who
may have shoved you into a certain "acceptable" way of
presenting yourself and having an "acceptable" set of values. But now
no one is constantly asking if you have a boyfriend or girlfriend. Your
grandma isn't constantly buying pink things for you if you're a girl
and athletic wear for you if you're a boy. It's your time to find your
true self in an environment where hopefully there is no judgement
at all. **Aside from the few people who are still stuck in their ways,
college is a place where gender does not define you, your sexuality
isn't a topic for gossip, and you can pretty much do whatever you
please.** (This is where all the parents reading this decide not to pass
this book on to their kids, assuming they didn't already decide that
after reading the friends with benefits chapter...)

Take advantage of this millennial acceptance and free your
mind. Wear the clothes you want to wear despite your brainwashed

assumption that they have to be the appropriate color, size, style, etc. If you're a girl and you want to ask the girl out who's been smiling at you all semester, do it. If you want to wear baggy t-shirts and men's clothing and you're not a man, do it. If you *are* a man and you want to wear a dress, do it. Wear men's clothing one day and a skirt the next; wear whatever makes you feel most like yourself. Now is your time to figure your own self out without the pressure of "established" societal views. You don't have to feel afraid. If you decide that you do not want to define yourself by or limit yourself to one sexuality, you have the freedom not to do that as well. We are granted one life to live, and you owe it to yourself to feel comfortable in your own skin and happy about who you choose to love.

It is also important to *be* one of those accepting young individuals. If your friend is going through a confusing time in their life, be there for them. Some people actually get kicked out of their homes for admitting to their true expression. Be there for people and give them a sense of comfortability. Everyone deserves that! It may be a hard adjustment for you if you come from a family who frowns upon different ways of life, but we need to support those around us and be the change we are all hoping for. **No one should be scared to be themselves.** No one should worry if what they are doing is pleasing to people around them.

Most importantly, you do not owe anyone an explanation for your actions. Finding yourself and loving who you choose to love is not anything that you ever have to explain. Believe me, people will ask what the hell is going on and where all of it came from. They will make you feel like you owe them an explanation, but *you absolutely do not.* You only have to tell your friends and family what you want them to know. Keep anything you wish to stay close to yourself close to yourself, and when people ask questions, tell them you are doing exactly what you want to be doing.

In my own personal experience of finding my own sexuality, I always kept to myself in most ways, especially in the beginning when I was figuring myself out the most. **The people you choose to love do not define who you are, either.** Although society really makes it seem like the end of the world for whatever reason, it's far from it. As you explore your sexuality in college, this does not mean it is concrete for the rest of your life. It means you are dating someone and that hopefully it will work out, but if it doesn't, you have not permanently cancelled out every other option. Or maybe you have, and that's fine, too. **Write your own story and try not to worry too much about what other people have to say about it.** Always treat people with kindness, for you never know what they are going through. Be the support system that someone may desperately need. **I encourage you to be exactly who you want to be. You will always find the right people who love you for you, even if you have to filter out a few who don't understand.**

Coming out to your friends and family is a step that some do not take until later in life. It is by no means easy to let people know what's going on in your life, especially when it involves who you're dating. The outcome may not be what you're hoping for, but hang in there. There will always be people around you who will take you in. Find friends who will be your home away from home. Embrace them and know that they will always be there for you through all of this.

I want you to remember that someone will always disapprove of something you are doing with your life; someone is bound to disagree with choices you make. How you react to that disapproval is what shows your true colors. Never forget that your happiness is worth just about anything! People who love you will always come around, even if it doesn't feel like that now. Spend time focusing on what makes you the happiest. I wish I had done this at some points in my life; I wish I would have only listened to myself and not others around me when they had no business getting involved in what I was doing.

Stay true to yourself and always remember that it is okay to change your mind. You are never stuck in any dynamic—you have the ability to change anything at any time. Life is not a scripted story! You write your own individual storyline. **What's important is that you are happy, you feel free, and you are embodying the best version of yourself.** Be patient with those around you and be confident in who you are. You are a frickin' superstar, and you owe it to the world to be your true self at all times!

CHAPTER 16

Staying Healthy

A LTHOUGH FRESHMAN YEAR WAS A HEALTH WAKE-UP CALL for me, it was around my sophomore year when I realized that staying healthy in college is not an easy task. You are constantly knocking down your immune system with an unethically large amount of alcohol and surrounding yourself with an abundance of people at all times. Not to mention you are definitely not getting the right amount of sleep at night, most likely not drinking enough water, and only getting nutritive value out of scrambled eggs with cheese. Due to all of this, you are either always sick, breaking out, and/or constantly feeling exhausted.

Although it's probably the last thing on your mind, staying healthy is more important than you think during these stressful times. Energy levels can sometimes be the make-or-break factor of whether you do well in your classes. It's nearly impossible to pay attention to a two-hour-long lecture when you have a cold or feel under the weather. Plus, feeling lousy gets in the way of going out with your friends, getting your work done, and really doing anything important. You will find that when you feel energized and healthy, your days are more productive and you look forward to getting things done. Below are some commonly known but most commonly forgotten tips to stay healthy and shine bright during your four years of college.

1. Wash Your Damn Hands

It wasn't until I started dating a germaphobe that I realized washing your hands more can actually save you from getting sick all the time. *Always* wash your hands before you eat. Wash your hands before and after working out. Every single time you get home from class, give your hands a nice scrub-down. Obviously wash your hands after you use the bathroom and *always wash your hands when you get home from a frat party.* You should probably throw your sweaty self in the shower after those parties, too, but by now we know that doesn't always happen.

Do yourself a favor and keep your hands clean. That is a simple act that can save you from a ton of small viruses and save you a lot of urgent care visits and class skips. And along with washing your hands, *keep your hands away from your face!* Make a habit out of this at all times. Touching your face with germy hands can result in some pretty serious illnesses. Avoiding touching your face and always making sure you wash your hands will keep you healthy and will result in no class skips. You'll want to save your skips for when it gets warm out, not waste them on being sick.

2. Exercise

If you are feeling like there is nothing you can do to work up any energy anymore, it's not because you are getting old. Exercising for at least 30 minutes to an hour a day will completely alter your energy levels. Aside from trying to lose the Freshman 15, working out will benefit you in many other ways: you will start to see improvements in your skin and in your motivation and energy levels, and your sleep patterns will normalize despite the nights you stay out until 5 a.m.

At-home workouts can do the trick, but getting outside and walking to your campus gym will allow you to also meet people. I met a ton of my close friends from spending time at the gym! This will motivate you to make time in your day for exercise, because not only do you want to go and work up a sweat, you also want to go see your friends. The campus recreational center will most likely have some type of classes that will also help you get in shape.

It's super important to focus on improving yourself both physically *and* mentally. Do not ignore this! You will actually see a change in your day-to-day mood if you stay active. When you work out, your brain releases serotonin, and although you may not feel its effects immediately, good serotonin levels will enhance your mental health. *Stay active!* Being active has so many benefits.

Finding time during college to work out feels like a huge task, I know. You feel like you have a thousand things going on—how could you possibly squeeze a workout into your day? But once you get on a routine and make it a priority to get to the gym a few days a week, you will feel a lot better about the productivity of your day, I promise. Staying active will make or break how you feel from day to day.

3. Eat

You would think this is common sense, but surprisingly, college comes with many bad eating habits and eating disorders. It's not always an easy thing to remember how important it is to eat well when you have a million other things going on, but making sure you are eating correctly can keep you from getting sick, keep your body fueled with energy, and improve your mood. The food you eat is your body's inner fuel. It's what your body operates off of. If you are anything like me, you may feel like you are barely eating but are nonetheless gaining weight every day. If we're being honest, it's the alcohol you are drinking, not the food you are eating. Sure, the dining hall options don't help your cause, but until you put the Four Lokos down, you'll never look like a fitness influencer. So instead of beating yourself up over that, let's talk about the basics. **You need to eat in order to survive.** Although you may feel better about yourself when you don't eat, you won't feel better about that in the long run.

As someone who has recovered from an eating disorder myself, I can assure you that *you need to love yourself for everything you are worth and never let other people's opinions of your body get to you, not even if it was once your significant other.* If you do not eat for many hours and then eventually eat only because you need to, your metabolism will be in shock and will hold onto the only food you finally did decide to eat. If you eat regularly, on the other hand, you will digest and metabolize food in a more beneficial way, and that will lead to maintaining a healthy weight. It's also true that if you do not eat much during the day, you are a thousand times more likely to eat half a pizza when you get home from a party that night. Spacing out your meals during the day is the best way to prevent yourself from drunken binge-eating at night.

Another fact that most young adults need to hear: throwing up your food does not get rid of the calories. I'm sure you are probably thinking of a TV show where a girl struggled with bulimia and suddenly lost a bunch of weight. This is a TV show for a reason. Not only does throwing up *not* undo the calories you have eaten, it has other consequential health issues tied to it. If you are constantly throwing up, you will damage your esophagus, your teeth, and your stomach lining. This is not worth fitting into those tight pants, so please do not think that throwing up is an option. And if you are thinking of a friend who does this and it's seeming to work, I'll let you in on a little secret: after they heal and stop regurgitating all of their food, *they will gain back double of whatever weight they lost.* Your body goes into shutdown mode and starts to hold onto every single calorie that stays in your system, resulting in massive weight gain. Bulimia is nothing to joke about! It's a real sickness that is way too common in college. Be kind to your body and be confident in your own skin—you will thank yourself in the end.

There are going to be drunken nights when you eat a whole pizza yourself and go to sleep directly afterwards, waking up with sauce still on your face and a major stomachache. Let yourself have these nights without beating yourself up over it. You are young— you have plenty of years ahead of you to look like a fitness model. Eat the pizza, wake up, and try harder the next day. By eating breakfast whenever you can, choosing healthier lunch options, and always eating dinner before you go out, you will start to see positive changes. Stay consistent in your workouts, and most importantly, *be patient with yourself.*

Struggling with self-love is something everyone falls victim to, whether they admit it or not. Spend time focusing on your favorite parts of your body and be confident in who you are. **Although it is easier said than done, love yourself.** Your body is no one else's body but yours, so take care of it and appreciate every single part of it. And remember, college isn't a time to be a fitness model unless you really truly aspire to be one as a career. So eat the pizza, drink the Four Lokos, and worry about shredded abs a little later. Just make sure that along with the pizza, you are eating nutritious meals that will fuel your body properly.

4. Give Yourself a Mental Break

As I've said many times, **give yourself a break.** You need to realize how much you have on your plate at all times. Sometimes it's healthy to take a day or even a few hours to not think about that plate at all. Whatever you love doing—writing, painting, drawing, etc.—make time for that. Make time to meditate or just lie on your floor for a few minutes. If you don't take some time here and there to de-stress, then stress will overcome you, and believe me, that is not a good feeling. If you have a park nearby, drive there with your favorite music playing and get away from your usual routine for a while. This doesn't mean you should neglect your responsibilities for a long period of time (unless you have to), *it just means take a minute to breathe.*

That being said, if you do need more than a day or an hour to breathe, it's vital to take that time. Your mental health is more important than anything else. People around you may not feel that way, but if you keep trying to push yourself and you ignore your mental status, you will eventually break. Let's prevent that! Get outside and walk around or lock yourself in your room for a while or do whatever works for you. **Reflect, breathe, and take the time you mentally need.**

If you feel like you can't do this alone, reach out to your resources. Your campus has people who are there for you at all times: your professors, school psychologists, wellness center staff, etc. These people are there to motivate you, give you that extra push you may need, and make sure you are doing well. Seeking help is NOTHING to be afraid of or ashamed of—everyone struggles with their own mental health issues. If you feel you need help and you seek it, that shows how strong you are.

5. Napping is Healthy

You are never getting enough sleep in college. If you can find the time to nap, even if it's 15 minutes in between classes, do it. Napping for a short amount of time can give you the extra boost you need to get through the day. It's not unhealthy to catch up on sleep here and there. Napping for hours may mess up your sleep schedule, but if your body needs it, do it. Listening to your body's needs is super important in staying healthy. Make time to nap, even if it's just for a short amount of time per day.

The bottom line in staying healthy is knowing when to listen to your body. If you are hungry, eat. Eat foods that will fuel your body in positive ways but also know when it's okay to give yourself a treat. If you are staying active in the gym, know when to take a short break and give your body time to heal. Listen to your mental needs as well and make sure you are taking the time you need to move forward. **You will be killing the game if you constantly pay attention to yourself. Although college makes that difficult, do not ever put your own needs on the back burner.**

CHAPTER 17

The Holidays, Take Two

COMING HOME FOR THE HOLIDAYS THIS YEAR WILL most likely be just as exciting as it was for the past few years. For some of us, though, this means picking up extra shifts at work to buy our families gifts. Depending on how you celebrate your holiday, this could be pretty stressful. (Not to mention that you've also waited until the absolute last minute to start any of your holiday shopping.) You may not be expected to shop at all, but a small thoughtful gift for each family member is always a sweet reminder that they are on your mind despite your crazy world of college activities. Even though your parents might say that you coming home is the only gift they need, pick up a candle and a card or something anyway...and expect a huge thank you.

Growing up is strange around this time, because you're never sure when you have become an adult in your family's mind. Sure, they are asking how your pre-med track is going, but you may still have a spot at the kids table with your baby cousins. Sometimes families just never want their kids-turned-young-adults to grow up…in the best way, that is. Think of it as an advantage to sit at the kids table—you may not have to listen to your Uncle Greg talk about sports betting or your Aunt Cindy complain about her sciatica. Your baby cousin might be drooling, but at least he can't talk yet. Plus, sitting at the adult table allows more people to ask more questions about your future, and who wants that as a sophomore in college?

Being home for the holidays may bring some nostalgia back depending on how often you've been visiting home all along. This may mean old thoughts of your high school ex, friends you had in high school, or other people/things you've rightfully pushed into the past. **Remember that your time in your hometown is something to cherish but NOT always something to invite into your future**. If you are doing extremely well at school with new things and new people, what makes you think people from your past should be invited into your new life? Of course, that depends on how you left your hometown people and how they treated you, but remember, if they seem like they haven't changed, they probably won't be changing any time soon. So if you are lucky enough to read this while you're sitting at home on Christmas Eve, New Year's, or whatever occasion your family celebrates, *don't text your ex!* **Nine out of ten times, texting your ex is a waste of your energy.** Getting lunch with an old friend isn't a bad idea. Catching up and talking about where your lives are now is healthy and can be beneficial. Just remember how far you've come and don't let the feeling of being home put you back where you were two years ago.

While you *are* home, though, appreciate the quirky little things your family does to piss you off. You don't get to see them all the time anymore, so try not to explode when your dad tells a crappy joke or when your mom asks you to help her make holiday cookies.

These are times you will never get back, so cherish them and spend as much time with your family as you possibly can. Respect your parents even though you've been on your own for two years now. It may be hard to take direction from them, but don't forget that without them, you wouldn't be where you are today. Take your dog for a walk, take your brother shopping, and paint your sister's nails. **Be with them! They miss you more than you'll ever understand.**

Hopefully this is common sense to you, but in case someone needs to hear it: be kind to your family. If you fight with your siblings, don't drag it out further than it has to go. You only get one immediate blood family, and if you are lucky enough to have one, appreciate them. Chances are that if you are in college, your parents worked extremely hard for you to have that opportunity, so treat them with respect and love. Fighting with your family members comes along with being a family, sure, but remember who raised you and gave you the privilege to go to college to better your future. Even if your parents don't financially help you as much as they might wish they could, they still worked hard for you to be able to attend college.

Some people don't have the privilege of having a family or having more than one parent or guardian, so if you *are* lucky enough to have an expanded family, give everyone an extra hug and kiss. It may be hard to get used to your parents asking what you're up to again—after all, for the last year and some change, you didn't owe anyone an explanation. Just keep in mind that they are your parents and they are trying to keep you as safe as they possibly can. Parents wanting to protect their children is human nature. Don't get too upset about their questions. Instead, appreciate the fact that they care enough to look after you.

CHAPTER 18

Spring, We Meet Again

I T'S THE SECOND SEMESTER OF YOUR SOPHOMORE YEAR ... where the hell does time go? It's dage season again, and you are a few steps closer to being an *upperclassman*. With a little over two years left, you begin to truly consider your career path if you haven't already. It's around this time that your advisors are pushing you to pick a path, because if you don't, you may have to take extra classes. Remember that graduating on time will save you money ... but on the other hand, don't let this fact push you into a major you absolutely hate. If you still aren't sure what to choose, your college might offer classes like exploratory studies or random free electives that will help you decide. Take advantage of your resources and dive deep into what you can see yourself doing. **Do your research and weigh out your options! The world really is your oyster at this point.**

If you haven't picked a major yet, chances are most of your classes are still relatively easy. Appreciate this, because believe me, that doesn't last forever! The positive aspect of having an easy course load is having time to spend on trying to decide what you want your next semester to look like. Signing up for clubs or going to organizational fairs will help you decide where you can see yourself. Write down things you love to do and decide what profession offers the most of those activities. *Anything* helps at this point.

Do not expect making this decision to be easy, and do not expect that even if you decide on something, you will be absolutely sure about it. Most people are never actually absolutely sure about what they have chosen. You will always have thoughts that maybe you picked the wrong major or maybe you would have done better in a different field. This is not the end-all, be-all! Remember that your future is about a lot more than your chosen career path.

If you have chosen a path with a broad field choice, you may not receive the best feedback from others. Everyone seems to have their own opinion about successful career paths, but the truth is that *you only need to listen to yourself.* Liberal arts studies, communication studies, etc. can set you up for an extremely successful future. Look at stories of extremely successful business owners who went to school for art...or famous people who never went to school at all. (Or authors who slid by with a Communication Studies degree... *cough.*) Get the degree, build your résumé, and put yourself out there. Once again, choosing a degree does not negatively impact your future career path. As if I haven't said that enough.

In a sense, I started to write this book so that I could stress to incoming college students that being in college is already being a step ahead. People don't stress enough to you that your path does not end with choosing a major. Or that picking a field does not limit you whatsoever to that specific area of study. (And I continued to write this book when I realized there's a whole lot more I wish I had known when I was going through school.) Keep your head on your shoulders, network, and create relationships you can use in the future.

Never lose your sense of determination. Employers care less about your degree and more about what you have to offer. By networking and making connections, you can set yourself up for the best opportunities. When I was a sophomore, I cared more about picking a degree than going to campus events to meet employers, but now I know I should have focused more on my surroundings and the resources I was given to succeed. Don't stress about which degree to get—focus on getting one and making connections.

By mid-semester, you are probably planning spring break again if you can afford it. Refer back to those spring break survival tips and stay safe. Be smart, create memories, and once again, don't underestimate the power of alcohol! If you've decided to take a bench spot this year, utilize those ten-plus free days to focus on your own needs that you may have accidentally neglected over the past few months. Write more, create more, and give yourself time to explore your passions. College is a time to find yourself, so take this time off of school to do so.

The Return of Finals Week

Finals are here again! Although this time you know what to expect, that doesn't make it any easier. Frankly, finals only get harder the more advanced college gets, so the only way to manage this is to find which study methods work best for you. During my college career, I always focused on the final I had coming up first and studied as hard as I could for that one; once it was over, I worried about the next final. Prioritizing your time will help the workload seem less heavy. Or perhaps you may find that you like to study for all of your finals each day. Go with whatever tactic makes you feel the most confident. As I said before, take finals seriously—often, they make or break your grade. Give it your all, remember to eat, and keep in mind that when they are over, you'll have a long summer of no schoolwork...hopefully, at least. **Be confident in what you are capable of, stay positive, and don't let your workload intimidate you. You got this!**

At every university, finals week brings perks that some students forget to take advantage of. There is almost always free food and free coffee in the library during these times, for example, or even events during the day that take the stress load off. My school provided a stress-relief puppy play center during finals where we got to play with puppies. Although it may seem hard to manage your time *and* get out there to take advantage of what your school is providing, I suggest you try to make time to do so. Grab a free coffee and take a breath! Your school is there to make things easier for you, so take full advantage of that.

CHAPTER 19

Summer Fun

WELL, YOU DID IT—YOU GOT THROUGH TWO WHOLE years of college! Despite everything standing in your way, you barreled through. On the bright side, you are halfway through the schoolwork and the pressure. On the downside, you are two years closer to the real world. But more importantly, it's summer! You've been waiting for a chance to breathe. How you spend your summer is completely up to you, but of course I have advice for you.

Finding a summer job and saving up as much money as you can will most definitely help you in the long run. It will allow you to experience things in the future that you may have never been able to afford otherwise. Working in the summer will improve your work ethic, teach you life lessons, and put you in a place to make future connections. By working and saving up money during the summer, I was able to not work as hard during the school year and focus on finishing my degree. Although working in the summer isn't ideal, it becomes almost a necessity. Give it your all in your early years of college summers!

I also encourage you to work hard now to prepare for a future summer when you may decide to do an internship. Summer internships can be unpaid but extremely beneficial to both your résumé and your future networks. However, as a college student, you probably can't fathom working for free, so take this summer to make up for the next. Plus, summer jobs can also be extremely fun if you get along with your co-workers. You'll make friends, learn a lot, and make enough money to enjoy yourself at concerts or do other things you enjoy.

Depending on how you did thus far in college, you may find that you are forced to take summer classes. I'm not going to sugarcoat it—*that sucks*. However, the majority of students end up having to take at least one summer class during their college career, so don't sweat it. Take advantage of having the time to purely focus on one or two classes. This will boost your GPA and help you get just a little bit closer to your major completion. But a word of warning: before committing to summer classes, make sure you have the financial means to do so, because financial aid will not help you during the summer. If you do end up having to take summer classes, it is vital that you do well in them. You do not want to pay out of pocket for a class or two that you can't use towards your degree. Study hard and do not expect these classes to be easy.

Having said all of this, summer is your time to relax, so don't overwork yourself. Make time to do things for yourself. If you have the time and money to travel, go see the world! This can teach you a ton about life and allow you to make connections. Some other cool options for your summer are teaching abroad or doing an internship in another country. If you never got the chance to study abroad, doing it in the summer is a great option. Take your summer to see the world, expand your horizons, and self-progress.

Being able to choose exactly how you want to spend your summer is the beauty of independence. But whatever you choose, place yourself in a progressive environment, which is to say while you're making time to have fun and be young, also make time to build yourself.

PART THREE
FEEL OLD YET?

CHAPTER 20

Junior Year

HOLY SH*T, HOW HAVE YOU COMPLETED THE WHOLE first two years of your college career?? You are now old—you're an upperclassman and you've made a name for yourself. Hopefully with my advice in mind, a good name. However, in the grand scheme of things, it doesn't matter if you did or didn't just as long as you are happy. **Buckle up and hang in there! The next two years are going to be the most influential time of your life.** You have *so* much to look forward to in the next two years that I can only attempt to cover all of it. Somehow, your last two years in college will make more of an impression than the first two. This is your growing period, when you'll learn a ton about yourself and the world around you. In the best way, of course.

You have most likely moved off campus into a house or an apartment that you pay your own rent for. *Yikes.* Now are you seeing where I was coming from when I said work your ass off in the summer? Hopefully you get along with your new roommates and you are getting acclimated to a space that doesn't belong to the campus. There's a lot to get used to here. If you are lucky enough, you may have your own driveway this year; if you don't, you'll most likely have parking right outside your apartment, which is still nice. You'll also have bills—welcome to the real world! Utilities add up more than you ever realized they would, and rent is through the roof. You have to swallow this all at once, and it's a big bite! Take a breath, get a job that you can handle along with your schoolwork, and take all these new responsibilities head-on. You've mentally prepared for this.

Welcome to budgeting

During my junior year, I had to juggle finances, including gas, rent, utilities, dues for a sorority, loan payments, etc. In order to do this, I had to budget…which is what I am now going to explain to you how to do. Budgeting will be the key for your financial stability. If you can organize and manage your finances, you will find it easier to manage everything around you. This will prevent you from falling behind and ensure that you stay afloat. If you are lucky enough to have your parents' or someone else's financial help, you can skip this section. If not, *hang in there—I am going to help you out.*

Step One: Get a Budget Notebook
You are probably thinking, "A *notebook*? Yeah, right…" But getting a budgeting notebook will help you manage your finances and keep them all in one place so that you don't mix anything up. That's very important! This may seem like an extra step, but you'll thank me later. You can also make a budget section in your planner *(which I know you ended up getting)* that you can refer to. Your finances are

personal, so make sure that wherever you write them down, you keep them to yourself. You do *not* want anyone else to see this information! Make sure you write it down in a place that only you can access.

Step Two: Write Down Your Monthly Income

Write down your income *every single month*. When you get a paycheck or see a mobile deposit, write it down. Create a new page for every month and keep track of exactly how much you make that month. If it's your birthday month and people give you birthday cash, write down that money, too. *Any* source of income you come across—even a $10 bill you found on the ground—write it down. This is my favorite part of budgeting and will obviously be yours, too. Who doesn't like continuously adding numbers up when it involves money?

Step Three: Deduct EVERY Expense

You'll have certain expenses that you know will occur each month, and you know exactly how much they'll be. You can write those at the top of the page, because you know that every month you'll have to deduct those from your monthly earnings. It sucks, I know. For expenses that may vary (like utilities), round up the amount you expect it to be or wait until your bill comes in. After writing down and deducting *every* expense you know you have to pay for, you'll end up with some extra spending money. Hopefully.

You'll have to write down every time you eat out, every time you buy coffee when you don't make it at home, and every time you have extra little expenses like getting new shampoo. It seems excessive to do this, but it can really help you stay on track with money. Nothing is worse than thinking you have an extra $100 in your bank account only to find out that you spent it on grocery shopping and a parking ticket. **Write every little thing down.** Again, keep this information private. You don't want anyone else knowing how much money you spend at McDonald's daily, anyway.

Step Four: Keep Track of Your Spending/Backup Money

Keep in mind that your spending money might need to be used in an emergency situation. For an example, I had once accumulated a few hundred extra dollars throughout the previous few months, and I was looking forward to spending it on a vacation. Then all four of my tires needed to be changed, so instead of going to Jamaica, I had to buy four new tires. Or maybe you decide to buy a new pair of shoes just to come out of the store and find an expensive parking ticket on your car. *Always* keep some backup money! Don't blow all of it on new shoes or plane tickets.

After you write down your monthly earnings and deduct your expenses, carry your extra money over to the following month and add it to your monthly earnings. This is also a happy part of budgeting! Adding is great when it involves money in your account. But remember that although having extra money can mean having spending money, you'll still have those monthly expenses to pay for next month. Things can happen with work (you may not get as many hours, for example), or if you are as fortunate as I was, you may end up needing work on your car. Be smart with your money and learn how to treat yourself in moderation. Most importantly, remember that a safety cushion can be extremely helpful in the long run.

Figuring out a work/school balance

Now that you have your finances under some kind of control, let's talk about other forms of adulthood. Getting a job that you can manage along with schoolwork and other newfound responsibilities can be hard. Sure, you can work somewhere on campus to make things extremely manageable, but for some of us, that's not enough money to pay for our monthly expenses. **The key to finding a good job that's flexible enough for your schedule is asking your fellow classmates where they work.** If they can juggle it there, chances are you can, too. An ideal student job is at a big company that knows you are a student, because they will most often be understanding about scheduling when you are giving them your availability. (In contrast, juggling a restaurant job can be very beneficial financially, but the long hours may make it hard to balance working at a restaurant with getting your schoolwork done.) Find what's best for you. If you have a major that doesn't allow for too much free time, look into working for their department on campus. Any way you can get involved on campus will also help your future employment opportunities. Do all you can now to make yourself marketable, because believe me, those last two years will fly by faster than you were expecting!

Figuring out your major

Hopefully you've decided on a major by your junior year, or at least settled into a general field that you enjoy. Take this and run with it! Find clubs according to your major and hold some sort of position in them. Find a part-time job that will give you relevant experience.

This is your time to start laying down the pavers of your future. You may not have thought about this as much as a freshman or sophomore, and that's fine. (I even suggested that you put off doing so.) But *now* is your time to build your résumé, make yourself marketable, and dive deep into preparing for the real world. It's important that you take this time to give it all you got—you are only going to be in your college bubble for a few more years. **You are determined and brave and will make an amazing employee one day! Now is the time to prove that.**

Academic advisors are there to help you

One resource you need to adhere to during your junior year of college is your academic advisor. You are lucky enough in college to have people around you who can tell you what your next steps should be. Your academic advisor is someone you must continuously and often see if you expect to graduate on time. Your advisor will tell you the classes you need to take, how many credits away from graduation you are, and most importantly, if you are on the right track. They will be your most valuable resource during your last two years of college. (If you have already switched your major a ton of times, you are probably familiar with how helpful advisors are.)

Next comes building your résumé and assuring that you are on the right professional track. Luckily, there are people for that, too. The office of career advancement (or whatever your university may call it) will be a great resource for you during the last few years of college. They will help you organize your résumé, assist in mock interviews, and even at times provide you with professional clothing if you do not own any. You will see this place mostly during your senior year, but it doesn't hurt to become familiar with it early on. Getting ahead of the game during your last two years is not a bad thing!

Finding a job that will help your future

By the time my junior year came about, I barely had an idea of what I wanted to do for the rest of my life. I had found a student job with Red Bull, it was fun, and I met most of my good friends at my job. Not only did I enjoy it, it gave me a bunch of professional experience to talk about in future employment interviews. **If you are lucky enough to find something that's beneficial in multiple ways, stick with it.** Once you do find something that will better your future, dive deep and make yourself stand out in any way possible. Take on extra responsibilities, be there as much as you can for your coworkers, and always show that you are trying to go above and beyond. Create and maintain good relationships with your boss, people higher up in the company, and everyone around you. **Networking at work events will take you far! Take advantage of this.**

You also need to keep in mind that if you find yourself at a job you absolutely hate, find another one. This is most likely an unpopular opinion—everyone else will tell you to stick with it and wait for it to get better. But as I said at the beginning of this book, I am here to tell you the raw facts, not what everyone else is telling you. Life is short, and working a job you hate going to at this age is a waste of your time. Thousands of companies would love to hire you, new places that will give you a chance to grow.

If you are unhappy where you are now, no one else is going to change that but you. It may be stressful to completely drop something you have been involved with for a while or even something you just started, so find another job before you quit your current one. **You may have to start over in terms of the totem pole, but your happiness is worth just about anything. You must not forget that.** Having a "good" job at this age is not worth being unhappy. Appreciate the time you had there and move forward knowing that better times will come. **You need to keep in mind that you will only reach that "better" when you let go of what's making you unhappy.**

The nuances of internships

At this point in time, internships become a topic of conversation. People have either already had them, currently have them, or plan to have them in the upcoming semester. Internships can be extremely helpful for finding future employment. Applying to an internship is your first step towards adulthood and the professional world. The company you intern for might even actually hire you full-time after graduation.

There are tons of internship opportunities, but unfortunately, a lot of them are unpaid. (*I'm not sure in what world **not** paying college students to work became acceptable...*) But there are also paid internships! I suggest you scroll through those and apply to them first. That said, if you find an unpaid internship to be exactly up your alley, it isn't the worst idea. In fact, it isn't a bad idea at all—you just need to make sure you have enough money saved up to focus your time on an unpaid position. They are often only a few hours a week, making it manageable to fit in with classes and another (paid) job if need be.

Internships can be found in many fields other than your own, so do not be afraid to search outside the lines. You may be pleasantly surprised and fall in love with another line of work. As long as you can apply your skills, an internship will benefit you tremendously. You can find one online or just by word of mouth. As I said before, networking can take you far. If you have a connection with someone who works for a company that hands out internships, it never hurts to ask them about it. (And once you do land your first internship, know where you stand in that department and remember that you have to start somewhere.)

It is also smart to find a job that involves professional work you can use on your résumé; at times, this can replace an internship. If you are already working for a huge company, there is not much reason to stack an internship on top of that. It would be more beneficial to start asking for extra responsibilities within that company. Remember that what you put on your résumé will benefit you regardless—as long as the skills can be applied to many professional settings, it will not matter if it's a job or an internship.

... But you're still a college student!

So you've explored internships, major choices, and career opportunities and now you just need a fuc*ing break. Deciding whether to intern for a huge company or get a job on campus has been your main thought for an entire week, and you are sick of it—your friends are going out, but all you can think about is the next step in your career. I'll tell you what you need to hear: *go out and enjoy your time as a young college student.* You may think that you are old now that you're an upperclassman, but you are absolutely *not.* The last two years of college will feel like premie years pretty soon, so enjoy still having times when you don't come home until 5 a.m.

Dressing up and getting ready to see a bunch of people you won't ever see again in a few years is something you need to hold close to you at this point. Appreciate these times! Make memories that you won't ever forget and worry about your career path when you wake up.

All throughout college, you'll feel like you need to know exactly what you are going to be doing for the rest of your life. I wish someone would have sat me down in those days and explained to me that I couldn't get that time back. (I couldn't be drunk and ordering French fries at 4 a.m. for much longer before people started to worry, for example.) Take this time as a junior in college to reflect on how important each and every night is. The people around you may be in your life forever...or they may not. Don't take them for granted. Spend as much time with them as you can, because you never know where your paths will take each of you.

The here and now

If you're as neurotic as I was in college, you'll wake up and realize although you have nothing to do that day, it is your duty to get on your computer and search for "A Day in the Life of a [fill in the blank]." You need to research what *exactly* this job entails. You've been thinking about this career choice for some time now, and you can't help but to shoot up from a deep sleep and check it out. Treat yourself to a cup of coffee (or tea if you don't drink coffee). Breathe for a minute and focus on the tasks you have right in front of you. Then research what exactly has been on your mind.

I'll tell you one thing: what was on my mind my junior year of college was completely different than what I decided to pursue in my later years, so take this advice with a grain of salt. Focus on what exactly it is that you must do for the class ahead of you, your class tomorrow, and so on. *Getting too far ahead of yourself is one of the worst things you can do at this point,* at least in some sense. Live in the moment. Focus on the things you have to do in the current day, and when you're done thinking about that, *then* worry about what your future is telling you to do. **Do not forget you still have another whole year ahead of you before you should start even considering what your plans will be after school.**

By this point, you should know how much can change within a year. If someone had told me a year ago that I would become an author, I would have laughed at them and continued to search for the career I thought I was destined to have. For some reason, we all tend to think we are destined to do *one* specific thing. But what if we are destined to do a lot of different things? That life search for our destined path may never be fulfilled if we limit ourselves to a singular choice. You, too, are destined to find yourself doing a bunch of different things. Your junior year, you may be thinking you want to go into marketing…and then by the time you graduate, you are only interested in business administration.

Your first step to becoming successful is getting a degree, and you are in the running for that. Know that after your degree is completed, you will go on to shine in many different ways. You will find that you love something so much that you actually start to make money doing it. You will also try new things and find out they just aren't for you. Be proud of how far you have come and focus on the important fact that you are one step ahead of the game! Worry about where your life is headed later on. I promise, you will discover what you are meant to be doing.

CHAPTER 21

Twenty-Fun

DEPENDING ON WHEN YOUR BIRTHDAY FALLS, YOU MAY be turning 21 around this time. You are about to enter a chapter in your life that you may have never explored before: *the bars.* The bars are a place for socializing that does not consist of a dirty, soggy basement on campus. It's a more mature setting that takes some getting used to. With being 21 comes responsibility, the expectation of being an adult, and a whole lot of fun. I always thought there was an unsaid line between being under 21 and over 21, because the people who were over 21 got to all bond over being allowed in bars. Believe it or not, this can be a big deal for a lot of people—they'll treat you differently once you cross that line of adulthood. Your 21st birthday may be slightly blurry in hindsight, but before you go on this adventure, below are some tips for surviving the night.

#1 Eat All Your Meals

Trust me when I tell you that eating a full, balanced meal for break-fast, lunch, and dinner can be the deciding factor as to how much you remember of your 21st birthday. This night is special! You are going to want to take away some memories from the night. Eat a good amount of carbohydrates and fuel your body with what it needs for the night ahead. Although it's your birthday and you may be eating cake today, try to get some greens in your body, too, to help avoid nausea.

#2 Stick to *One* Kind of Liquor

It's your birthday, and everyone around you will be buying you shots, drinks, beers, etc. It's going to be hard to stick to one type of alcohol, but if you do not want to throw up before the night even really starts, I suggest you at least try to stick to *one* category of liquor. If you give up on this tip towards the end of the night, you'll at least possibly make it to the bar and then home before you let your dinner go.

#3 Drink Water

This means all day long AND while you're out at the bar. Drinking water, as I've said before, can be the deciding factor for your body's longevity. Your body needs fluids to digest all of the alcohol you will be putting into it. Trust me, you will thank me later! Drinking water all day will help you the most at the beginning of the night, and having a cup of water between shots will help you make it through the rest of the night. Be smart! Like I said, you will want to remember this night.

#4 Take Pictures

The taking-pictures thing may be overwhelming tonight, but just remember that you are the star and therefore people will be constantly taking videos and pictures of you throughout the night. My advice here is to make sure you take some of your own pictures or have someone who is close to you take them and then send them to you. The pictures and videos that other people take may never get back to you, and you are going to want to look back on the night. Pictures and videos will help you recollect how your night went! Make sure you get enough of them.

Remember, *it's your night*. You can be as obnoxious and as ridiculous as you'd like to be for at least one night of the year. Your 21st birthday will be hyped up, and you'll most likely be more excited in the days leading up to it than you will be after it. Embrace this, be safe, and make sure you follow my tips so that you have some mental memories *and* actual photos to look back on. Pace yourself on your 21st birthday and don't forget that slow and steady wins the race.

CHAPTER 22

Comparing Ourselves

I FELT THIS TOPIC WAS WORTH AN ENTIRE chapter because we all struggle with comparing ourselves to others at times, especially in our later years of college when everyone seems to be so productive. It's human instinct to compare yourself to others—it feels natural to do. **Do whatever you can to NOT do this.** It is not a healthy thing to compare your successes to other people's successes! (Or really to compare anyone to anyone else, for that matter.) Everyone is living their own timelines and experiencing their own personal successes, including you. **The more time you focus on the different lives around you, the less time you spend on progressing your own.**

Although it may seem upsetting to think about your close friends doing big things, it may just not be your time to do those things. (Yet.) We need to agree to stop comparing ourselves to people who are pursuing a different journey than we are. (It's like looking at the success of a professional soccer player and wondering why you aren't progressing in your own acting career.) You need to know that focusing on your *own* success is the only way you will truly get better at anything you are doing. Asking other people how they are reaching their goals is healthy, but be sure to build off that in a positive way. The difference between taking advice from others and comparing yourself to them is that taking advice is a positive, helpful action, whereas comparing is more of a negative drain on your own success.

Avoid paying too much attention to the way other people live their lives and instead focus on the way you are living your own. It's especially important to do this during the last two years of college, because that's when everyone is working on setting up their individual futures. **My best piece of advice is to just focus on yourself during this time and work hard to improve your own life.** Do not let the progression of others hinder your own goals. Continuously remind yourself that you are your own person and that other people's successes or failures do not impact your own end results.

CHAPTER 23

The Motivation You Need at This Time

J UNIOR YEAR IS A TIME FOR PROGRESSION—THIS IS your time to make yourself as marketable as you possibly can while also maturing into a young adult. Like I've said before, this can occasionally all get to be too much. You need to focus on things that inspire you during these times, so take the time to read a motivational book or an article online. Empowering words can do a lot more for you than you may think! It's okay to admit that you've hit a wall when it comes to motivation and that you need a little extra push. Here are a few things to keep in mind when you are hitting a blockade to inspiration:

You Become Who You Think You Are.

During your years of college, you create an image of who you are and who you will eventually become. By keeping a positive mindset about these aspects of yourself, you will always progress. You are a rockstar, and you will continue to grow into the person you have always hoped to become. If you see something that you want to become, you *will* achieve that goal. Keep this fact close to you throughout college and throughout life. *You* are the creator of your own success. You owe it to yourself to keep your goals in sights at all times and work hard towards becoming what you wish to become. Know what you want and know that you have the ability to reach your goals. Always remember that the people you look up to started out where you are now. They got to where they are because they believed in themselves.

You Are a Reflection of Those Around You.

Your friends mean a lot to you—you have spent a ton of time together and share memories you may never forget. You may have gotten involved with people who have the same goals as you do. They help motivate you and they provide advice; together, you are rising to the top. On the contrary, you may have found yourself involved with people who are going to school just to say they went and are barely getting by. Although being friendly with the less-than-optimally-motivated is perfectly fine, it is important that you establish the difference between friends and people who are going to help you progress. Whether you notice it or not, the people you surround yourself with stand as a reflection of who you will become. You will unintentionally adapt the same mindsets, morals, and habits. Be aware of who you are spending your time with! If you feel that they are going in the opposite direction of where you wish to go, reconsider how much time you spend with them.

Struggle is Temporary and Beneficial.

Struggle is something you have become familiar with. It may not seem to be beneficial when it happens, but as you've commonly heard, what doesn't kill you makes you stronger, a clichéd quote that holds a lot of truth. The struggles of your college years will carry on into your adulthood and will strengthen your capabilities, and the amount of what you can handle will become greater and greater.

You also have to remember how temporary struggle is. What you may consider life-changing at this age will turn out to be temporary—whether it's financial, academic, or social, your struggle will come to an end eventually. Don't lose sight of the light at the end of the tunnel during these hard times. You'll keep these battles with you as life lessons, and how you overcame them will assist in your personal growth. Take your struggles as a blessing and remember that without them, you would not be able to progress.

Success Does Not Know Fate.

It is vital to know that your success is solely based on your actions. Fate does not play a part in how you achieve successes in life. If you want to be something or have something, you must go out and get it yourself. Sitting around and waiting for the perfect opportunity is not a valid plan. You must take each action seriously. When you do, every step gets you closer to success. Fate and success are *not* friends—they do *not* operate together. It is important to remember that *you are the determining factor in your future*. Nothing you achieve is predetermined destiny. Although it is comforting to believe that fate has a plan for us, it is realistic to know that success will not come to you if you do not go out and seize it yourself. You are fully capable of this.

Everyone Great Started at Square One.

Something we all subconsciously struggle with is looking at someone successful who has completed many (extremely arduous) detailed steps to get there and then wonder why *we* can't achieve the same thing. It's almost like we feel that that thing is out of reach for us but somehow came easily to them. This goes back to comparing ourselves to others, which we should never do. That said, it's easy to see someone at the top and assume we are not good enough to reach the same place. Delete that thought immediately! Get rid of the thought that you are incapable of attaining what other people have already achieved!

Every single person who is currently successful in their field started from at square one. Sure, some may have started at a higher point than others, but success is not easy to achieve for anyone. The accomplishments of celebrities or musicians may seem worlds apart from your current accomplishments or what you are capable of accomplishing. This mindset needs to be dismissed—you owe it to yourself to set your own expectations high. If you want to be famous, you absolutely can be. If you want to be a doctor, lawyer, or school principal, you can absolutely can be.

Of course, success is not going to happen overnight, just as it didn't happen overnight for those who are there now. Embrace the journey to success and know that no matter how great they are now, everyone started somewhere. **Believe in your abilities, work hard for what you want, and know that we live in a world where thankfully anything truly is possible for anyone.**

The World is What You Make of It.

How you view day-to-day occurrences becomes your destiny. If you can keep a positive outlook on life, you will see a more positive world; if you constantly victimize yourself within the world around you, you will be nothing more than that. Yes, the world can and will be shitty at times—we all know that by now. But how you cope with this is how you are going to see things in the wake of those shitty times. Find light in the darkness in every aspect of your being. Create happiness where it is hard to find.

As you walk through life, you will eventually come to realize that going through the motions is going to become repetitive, but still, dance through life! Shine when things are dark and always find beauty in the ugliness. You are the pilot of your life on this planet and it is your job to keep flying forward. Your world will only be bright if you find light in every dark place—if you wallow in the darkness, your world will be dark. Grip this life! Show the world that you are in charge and make it a beautiful place to inhabit. Constantly radiating positive energy will make or break whether your path is bright.

Your Destiny is Infinite.

Coming to college, we all have the idea that we are going to come across *one* major, *one* career path, *one* set of ideals that is going to fulfill our sense of destiny. We choose a career path and constantly question if that's what we are meant to be doing. This can become an unsettling thought, and I'll tell you why: as humans, we do *not* have one singular destiny—we have multiple destinies. We are not put on this planet to do one single thing; we are not created to fulfill one singular purpose. Instead, we are born to showcase our multiple talents, bless the world with our various skills, and contribute to multiple aspects of society. Thus, as you pursue your college journey, I want you to remember that you are not in search of *one* thing you are going to be magically great at. You are in college to get a degree and then go on to use that degree to find an enormous amount of things you are wonderful at. You will come across things you never saw yourself doing! Not every actor, writer, scientist, or engineer sat down and convinced themselves that it was their destiny to be that person from the very beginning—many of them found their path by exploring life and maintaining an open mind. You find what you are great at through doing multiple different things. You find what you love through experiencing different things, including things you may hate. **Your life it is not a multiple-choice question! It is a piece of artwork in progress.**

Keep these motivational thoughts with you during stressful times. Write them down and constantly remind yourself of them. Do whatever it takes to keep going. We all need motivation here and there, so do not be afraid to admit that. It is how you actively deal with bumps in the road that will separate you from the rest.

Senior year is almost here!

You are so close to senior year that you can smell it. You can finally see the light at the end of the tunnel in terms of your college career. During your junior year, you've felt like you have been going through the same motions for years, and you just cannot *wait* to be done with schoolwork. At the same time, though, you don't want your college career to end, because that will mean leaving your friends and fun times behind.

All of this means that junior year brings with it an academically relaxed mindset. You'll notice it in your friends, your classmates, and everyone around you. At this point, you have all found the loopholes in your classes and how you can pass them without fully applying yourself. Do not let this get the best of you! And do not underestimate the ability of your professors to catch you off-guard. While I can't assure that you will apply yourself to your studies as fully as you did during your previous two years, I *can* tell you that your professors will notice when you are starting to slip, and that will affect your grade.

Participating in classes can mean getting the few extra points that will change your grade from a B to an A, so it's worth raising your hand every now and then. Even though you will most likely be taking notes on a laptop and finding yourself shopping online or looking at other classwork, as hard as it is, try to pay attention to what your professor is saying—more times than not, your professor will be talking about exam information, class guidelines, etc. You will want to stay involved in these conversations, because you never know when they will spring a pop quiz on you or assign homework that involves lecture material. As difficult as it may be to stay academically involved at this point, keeping your GPA up will be worth it in the end. And here's another bonus to that: keeping your GPA up now will allow for some wiggle room when senior-itus hits. Trust me, once you are a senior in your last semester, your "junior-itus" will seem nonexistent. It is smart to apply yourself now and keep your motivation up to prepare for the inevitable senior mindset that you will not be able to control.

Other aspects of college may become less serious to you as well during your junior year. Clubs or organizations on campus may be put on the back burner, but try to keep those as close to you as you can so that you can ultimately use them to your benefit. Stay active in school as long as you can, keep up with your résumé-builders, and push through your junior-itus. Creating a balance between partying, schoolwork, regular work, and the thousand other things you have on your plate can become exhausting, but balance is key. You do not want all your hard work of the previous years to go to waste! In terms of your GPA alone, if you got great grades during your first two years of school but you slack off during your last two, those first two years of hard work will have been for nothing. It is very hard to get your grade point average back up after it drops, so save yourself the trouble and give your junior year all you got.

In terms of continuing to give college your full effort, you have to think about how much you owe it to yourself to do so. **You owe it to yourself to make the absolute most of your four short years in college and to try your hardest.** Challenging yourself is healthy and is often something that is missed the most post-graduation. It sounds outlandish now, but as soon as you do not have exams or homework to apply yourself to, you'll wish you can go back just to apply yourself a little harder.

CHAPTER 24

Lessons I Learned the Hard Way

B Y THE TIME YOU HIT YOUR JUNIOR YEAR, you will have definitely learned some lessons the hard way. My college career was filled with lessons I had to learn firsthand, which is why I decided to write this book in the first place. We all go through our own personal struggles and hardships, but I'm hoping that some of yours may be prevented by learning from the times I went wrong. My goal is to make your life easier! That's why I've decided to list some mistakes I made during my college career and how I recovered from them:

#1 Getting a Puppy

You've finally gotten your own place off-campus, and the only thing missing from your humble abode is a four-legged friend. You've always dreamed of having a dog as soon as you were able to. Your classes may have calmed down slightly and you feel financially stable enough in the moment, so you jump the gun and adopt a puppy. For the first few days, you convince yourself that no, you haven't bit off more than you can swallow. Getting up early and feeding your new child on time isn't the worst thing in the world! It is *totally manageable...*

As the days go by, your puppy adopts a new attitude. This includes barking, going to the bathroom in the house, and eating your shoes, pillows, homework, etc. A puppy's rebel years last until they are about three years old. As a college student, whether you like to admit it or not, you do not have the time to train a puppy correctly. Getting a puppy will ultimately result in your parents taking on a new responsibility. In the worst case, it may mean giving the puppy away to a new family. Save yourself the heartache and get a fish! You can go to class/work/a party with a fish and they won't bark until your neighbors file a complaint.

I never considered a lot of things before I got a puppy. The first vet bill for just the first round of shots was over $100, and I knew there were more bills to come. My shifts were six hours long and my puppy had to go outside every hour. (When they are that little, their bladders can only hold so much.) Yelling at him for peeing inside felt wrong even though I knew I had to train him to pee outside. Basically, I couldn't give him the time a puppy needed during his first few months. And as barking became an issue, my neighbors became more and more angry. There was no way for me to control it, especially when I wasn't home. Puppies can also get sick, keeping you up the entire night before a huge exam and costing you even more money. Before you make the adult decision to take on a pet, take the adult initiative to think about what exactly a pet commitment entails.

I got my ten-week-old puppy the summer before my senior year. His name was Milo, and he was the cutest puppy I probably could have ever chosen. (I say "was" because he is no longer mine and his name is no longer Milo.) At the time of my decision, I had free time, financial means, and a fairly flexible job. During the first few days, the sheer effort of having a pet was masked by joy, attention from others, and the new sense of companionship I felt with Milo. I gave my little man everything I had to offer and fell completely in love with him. Then, as the days progressed, he began to throw temper tantrums like a toddler, barking whenever I left the house and getting up in the middle of the night *every single night.*

I became extremely tense when I realized that I might have just made an adult decision I couldn't handle. What 21-year-old wants to face the fact that they made the wrong choice? You've spent all this time trying to prove you are old enough to make decisions for yourself, and then you end up at a dead end and you have to make an impossible decision to fix things. I had to pass my puppy on to a family who had more time to raise him. Watching my little guy leave tore me into pieces, and that's a feeling I never want you to feel. Think before you take on responsibilities! That leads me to my next point.

#2 Taking on Too Many Responsibilities at Once

So you've got a job and you are doing great in school. You feel like you can handle another responsibility, whether that's another job, class, or club. There are times when you will feel like a superman/woman and you will convince yourself that you can handle a whole extra commitment. And at times, you may absolutely be able to handle it, yes. Never sell yourself short! However, something I struggled with was rationalizing what each extra responsibly entailed. I had a good-paying job already, but I thought I could squeeze in another one to save up some extra money. I ended up having to take time off from my first job, which made my boss pretty angry.

This also led to me *not* giving the other job I had just started my full effort. The end results? I got rid of the extra job I had taken on and caused extra headaches for myself.

If you are finally floating along nicely, do not put yourself back underwater unless it is completely worth it. Taking fewer hours at my first job resulted me getting in the same amount of pay from both jobs combined, but driving between the two jobs *and* taking classes put me in a worse spot than where I started. Always push yourself, but do not surpass your own limits of time management.

Not over-pushing yourself also applies to college credits. You may want to get a head start or catch up and take extra credits one semester, but before you do this, research the difficulty of and involvement with each course you plan to sign up for. Loading on a bunch of credits can result in not doing as well and then having some of them not count. You want to have enough time for other things in your life! It is good to challenge yourself, but the recommended credit load is not in place for purely whimsical reasons. Listen to your advisors and only take the courses you can handle. You will thank me later.

#3 Paying for an Extra Gym Membership

You are getting older now, and sweating in the same fitness center as the incoming freshman makes you cringe. You start to realize it smells and everyone around you seems five years younger. You also can't stand walking into your school gym and having to fight over machines the entire time, so you consider signing up for a gym off-campus. But paying $20 to $30 a month will rack up quickly, and you will start to regret your decision. Having an extra monthly payment for a space that has already been provided to you will ultimately piss you off. Off-campus gyms will come with contracts that will give you no choice but to follow through with your decision.

If your school gym is getting on your nerves, switch up the time you usually go. Chances are you will find that fewer people will be there at certain times, and *voilà!* Your problem will be solved for free.

During my junior year, I got bored with the campus fitness facilities and signed up for a kickboxing gym. This resulted in me spending nearly the equivalent of my monthly rent for just a few classes. There was a cancellation fee involved—you had to pay for the first month and for the equipment they gave you when you signed up. The entire thing ended up being a huge lesson, but I definitely took a financial hit for that lesson. I went back to the campus facilities and found a different time that worked with my schedule and assisted me with avoiding the freshman stench in the weight room. You can do this, too.

#4 Job/Internship Scams

This is something that continues to stay under the radar but that affects many innocent college students. Scamming is something that you should always look out for—it can be pretty financially devastating if you don't. Believe it or not, there are scammers out there who construct formal emails that appear to offer different job positions or internships. They will most likely email you with a job or internship that sounds absolutely perfect for your field of study. The hours will appear manageable and the pay will be excessive. This is a red flag! Do not look past it. When you receive any type of job offer, you must verify it with a phone call or an interview. **Do not buy unmarked checks! Do not give anyone any bank account information or personal information without verifying the company, meeting with them, and doing your research.**

I have known multiple students who became victims of this scam. They chose to see the best in people and assumed it was a real offer. It resulted in their bank accounts getting wiped out and law enforcement barely able to trace the scammer. Now that you know this, pass it on to everyone you know. **Throughout your years in college, you need to be on your feet at all times! Stay aware of your surroundings, both in person and on the internet.**

#5 Do Not Give Too Much and Get Nothing in Return

Throughout my entire college career, I did everything I could for each and every one of my friends. I paid for their food and bought them small gifts because I was thinking of them and was there for them always. I constantly acted as a support system and always made sure they had everything they needed. I always did this without expecting anything in return—I never cared if they did the same for me, because it made me feel good to be there for people. This is a great personal quality to have. However, you will eventually realize that you are the only person constantly giving, whether it's in the context of a romantic relationship or a friendship.

You need to take a step back sometimes and realize it shouldn't always be a one-sided situation. (And it's worth noting that your friends don't have to buy you material things for you to know that the relationship is *not* one-sided.) There was a point in time when I would have sacrificed anything for my friends ... only to realize that if I ever needed anything, they wouldn't be willing to give the same. The time you spend with and on your friends should be reciprocated. They should also be there for you and spend just as much time taking care of your needs. That's what a friendship/relationship is all about!

You cannot forget this. It's easy to overlook when you care about people, but do not let them walk all over you. In my own experience, it took someone else noticing how much I was doing for everyone else for *me* to realize that I wasn't getting anything in return. Make sure your friends are there for you just as much as you are there for them. If you decide to look past this, one day it will all catch up to you and you will feel emotionally drained. The people around you should be able to give *you* what you give *them*.

Making the Most of Your Junior Year

It is my greatest hope that you are enjoying your junior year of college! This year I hope you made new friends, went to new places, and explored your own aspirations. Junior year is the pre-trial period for closing out this whole chapter of your life.

I hope you are taking this time to reflect on and enjoy everything around you. You are growing up more and more every day and becoming an amazing human being who will soon be put to the test of adulthood even more so than you have been during the previous few years. This is your time to shine! It's your time to flourish in being young and appreciating every single moment. I hope you are trying new things and not dwelling on anything that happened in your past.

At this point, you should be used to your surroundings, and that makes your possibilities endless. New ways of life and new experiences should be teaching you how incredibly huge your life is. You may have found things you aren't so great at, but I hope you have also found things you never knew you were so awesome at! You should be involved in a few things on campus and you should have learned what taking on responsibility feels like. You are thriving during these times! You are experiencing what a lot of people never get the chance to experience. Sure, some days are worth complaining about, but you see the light in all of it. You know that this is a time you'll one day wish you could return to. I hope you are realizing how special a college experience is and realizing that getting through the stressful times means you come out even stronger than you were before. Junior year should have taught you that any obstacle in your way is worth getting over! With a little over one year left in your college career, you need to appreciate every single moment and every single experience.

I can't help but to feel proud of you—you've made it this far and you have so much to offer. You have become someone you never thought you could be and have overcome many challenges and roadblocks. Give yourself a pat on the back for making it this far! You are in the home stretch. With a few months left of your junior year, relish everything a little bit more. Take walks around your campus that you'll have to say goodbye to in a year. Spend time in the library just soaking in the place you've called home for the past few years. Sit outside and watch an intramural sports game with a few friends. Talk to your professors a little more and thank everyone who never let you quit. Do everything you can to get out and enjoy your last few weeks as a junior!

PART FOUR
SAYING GOODBYE

CHAPTER 25

Your Final Year

T HAT'S IT! YOU BLINKED A FEW TIMES, AND now you are
in your last year. Although you feel like a completely different person than you were when you arrived, it feels like just
yesterday you were moving into your freshman dorm. *(I told you
so...)* You had time during the summer to mentally prepare for the
fact that your college career is coming to an end, but that doesn't
make it any easier to swallow. Hopefully you had an eventful summer and spent time on yourself while also saving up some money.

Now it's showtime again. You are back at school, and this time,
you are the one who's expected to know what you are doing *even
though you may not.* Your classes will most likely be the hardest
they have ever been, but no worries—you will get through this.
Hopefully by this time you've moved into an apartment with people
you actually like and you are adjusting to a nice new place. There
are a lot of things to get used to during your first week back. Some
are great, like getting to be the first to choose your classes and

getting to leave for classes five minutes before they start because you know exactly where the classrooms are. But some things aren't so great, like feeling pressured to have a perfect résumé and completing your senior capstone classes. Your senior year will be even more of a rollercoaster than the last three were, *believe it or not.*

This year will show you that adulthood is not something to joke about and that you may have had it a little easier than you thought you did for the last three years. It's time to put on those grownup pants and get out there! You've lived at this same school for three years, but now it feels completely different: you are treated with more respect and you are expected to be on your A game at all times. **You are looked at as an adult.** There are a ton of things you need to pay attention to this year, as early on as you can. This is the year that thinking ahead is something you should most definitely be doing. It's like you're just a mile away from the finish line of a long, highly anticipated race. You owe it to yourself to finish out your college career stronger than ever.

This chapter will give you tips on what to look out for and what to prepare for as well as the motivation to give you an extra push. We are in this together! I promise you, you *will* make it to that finish line. You *will* be able to walk across the graduation stage and wave to your family. Unless, of course, you graduated the year I did and your graduation was halted. A huge lesson this chapter will cover is that you need to be prepared to adapt to just about anything…like a pandemic. Nothing puts a bigger stomping boot on your senior year than a worldwide pandemic that shuts school down for the rest of the year. This is not to say that your senior year will go the same way mine did—this is to assure that you need to cherish every moment and need to be prepared for anything that's thrown at you.

It was about halfway through the second semester of my senior year when I was told I would never return to a classroom again. I was crushed. Never in my wildest dreams would I have predicted something as catastrophic as a virus that would keep everyone inside indefinitely. Within your senior mindset, you may be thinking that it would be a dream to have all your classes switch to online—I was excited at first. That is, until I realized I had to actually give up my entire senior year, not just my classes. I had to watch my friends leave the town we had lived in for the past four years without even saying goodbye. I had to put all of my job interviews on the back burner because all anyone cared about was staying safe. I watched friends lose their internships/job opportunities due to employment limitations. Companies with positions they had been applying to for months were calling them to cancel their offers. It was an extremely sad time. Although I don't want to deviate too much here from giving you senior year advice, I do want you to realize that not every day is guaranteed. I want you to know that each moment of your last days at school should be appreciated, because you never know what this crazy world will swing onto you.

As you enter the real world, it's important that you realize that this giant rock we live on calls the shots for us at times. Whether it's ideal or not, we must constantly adapt to what this planet has planned for us. In my case, it was a super-contagious virus that caused mass hysteria right in the middle of my preparation for adulthood. Being able to adapt to challenging circumstances is one of the most important parts of becoming an adult. Personally and professionally, you will have to exhibit flexibility to all situations. Your employer will be putting you to the test every single day, but as long as you can adhere to their needs, you will move up fast. Just like how college puts you to the test every day, so will the real world…only this time, you'll have fewer resources to pull you out of the mud. Which is why I stress to you how important it is to be able to think on your feet and adapt to any condition. Not only do I want to talk you through your last year of school, I want to also set you up to succeed once you are finally *out* of school.

That being said, although you are considering plans for after graduation, it is important that you also keep up with what's right in front of you. During your first semester, you shouldn't be applying to jobs yet—you just need to focus on doing well in your classes. After all, you won't be able to move on to the next level without first passing all of your classes.

So let's talk about senioritis. Just as I had warned you earlier, within few weeks of your first semester, you are already feeling it: your motivation is slipping, your classes are difficult, and by this time, you have just had enough of people telling you what to do. You feel like you are treated like an adult when it sucks to be one but treated like a child when it matters. Sitting in class and listening to your professors becomes redundant, and you feel that you are so close to the end that you question if your GPA even matters anymore.

Trust me, it does! Your GPA will often be looked at by your future potential employers. This number could be the difference between you and another candidate getting the job. Giving in to your senioritis mindset would be like walking instead of running at the very end of a marathon you trained so hard for. By walking at the end, you are letting a bunch of other people pass you. Giving up should not be an option!

You've worked so hard to get where you are! You need to push through and give your last few months all you got. Keep your grades up, keep studying for exams, and continue to show that you're making an effort. In a few short months, you will be looking back at how hard you tried, and you do *not* want to look back and know that you could have done better. Continue to be active in your extracurricular activities, find new ways to build your résumé, and do not lose respect for your professors. Just because you are an adult now does not mean you get to treat your professors like they're your friends. They are your mentors—they have gotten you to where you are today, and until the very end, you should be thanking them for everything they have done for you. Keep pushing through! It will be over before you know it.

At times, senioritis comes along with losing interest in other college lifestyle activities. Especially if you go to a smaller school, by your senior year, you may feel bored going out with the same people and going to the same places, so you begin to distance yourself and find happiness in other things. During my senior year, I felt I had done everything on my campus that I could possibly do and I just couldn't wait to get out of there.

You may be thinking I'm crazy for saying that, because you are already cherishing every moment of being with your friends and being at school. If you are, that's great! Continue to live up your last year. If you are anything like me, though, I suggest you take a step back. Take a step back and realize that although you might just be going out with the same people to the same places, you will absolutely miss those times. I wish I would have stayed involved, continued to go out with my friends, and appreciated every single moment I still had at school. If you can stand it, *force* yourself to live in your college moment instead of trying to move on to other things. This is time you will not get back! Keep your good friends close—spend time with them and do the stupid things you think you are too old to do. Senior year doesn't last forever, and neither does having the excuse of being a crazy college student.

CHAPTER 26

Professional Preparation

ALTHOUGH YOU PROBABLY DID SOME OF THIS AT the end of your junior year, chances are you are now in full-swing résumé-building and job-searching mode. One of your classes may be helping you with all of this, but it's worth hearing about it from all angles. Between résumé-building, doing mock interviews, feeling the pressure of graduation, etc., you are at your boiling point. Breaking down exactly what you have to do makes things a lot easier. You are most definitely feeling overwhelmed at this point, but the tips and resources below will help you take a breath.

Office of Career Advancement

Your school may call it something different, but as I mentioned earlier, you should get to know your career assistance office well. This office has been provided to you to assist you with finding a success-ful path. The staff there provide mock interviews, résumé-writing help, and sometimes even professional clothing for your job inter-views. They are there to help you, and I suggest you take advantage of this.

If you have never visited your career assistance office before, that's fine, but it is in your best interest to start visiting it now. Make appointments with the staff, ask them questions, and retain every-thing they tell you. They are there to make things easier for you. They have been through application processes many times with students and can guide you through them. They may even have op-portunities for you to work with them or they may know of places that are hiring. These staff members are great connections to have!

When applying to jobs, you are going to need to construct a résumé and a cover letter. These documents should not be taken lightly. Ask your career center for help, find other resources that can also help you, and create the documentation you need to land your dream job.

Career Fair

Chances are that in prior years, you wondered why the upperclass-men were all wearing nice clothes on a certain day. Or why they were all lined up outside one of the buildings with folders and brief-cases. They were most likely all lined up to walk into a career fair that your campus had set up for them. Now it's your turn to suit up or throw a dress on! Career fairs are overlooked all too often. If you don't have a class that requires attending one, you may think going is a waste of your time. I would have thought that, too, until I had to go to a career fair for one of my classes. I always thought that we had enough online resources and that I didn't necessarily need to go walk around in a gymnasium to meet future employers.

I was wrong. I'm here to tell you that yes, a career fair is worth going to. The employers who attend a career fair are most likely preparing to hire college graduates in the spring, so meeting them can be very beneficial. This goes back to what I was saying about networking, namely that it's absolutely vital. You must do everything you can your senior year and beyond to create and maintain connections with corporations and professional people. **Think of it this way: college is the ticket, but your connections are the train that will take you where you need to go.** You can't board the train without a ticket, and you can't get where you need to be without the train. My advice to you is to go to these career fairs. Actively present yourself and collect all the information you can. Get business cards and send follow-up emails to your top choices to make sure they remember who you are. Although you still have some time before you will be applying for jobs, keep these connections close so that *they* will be waiting for *you* when the time comes.

Career fairs are held outside of college campuses as well. Most of the time they are free, and these can be even more helpful to your professional growth. **Do not be afraid to put yourself out there, and remember that everyone at these events is waiting to board the same train.**

Résumés

Nothing is more frustrating than writing your résumé. Every person who looks at it will tell you something different than the last person did. You've worked so hard to build up your résumé with experience and extracurriculars, but now you are supposed to fit it all onto one page… Do not get discouraged—you will eventually have an award-winning résumé to show off to future employers.

The skills on your résumé should match up pretty well with the skills requirements for each job you apply for, so make sure you are editing accordingly. Your résumé is a piece of paper that is *why* you did most of what you did. You only joined the culture club to be able to validly include it on your résumé. You only stuck it out at a job you didn't enjoy to include it on your résumé. If you think about it, going to college was all about being able to just write it down on that same piece of paper. *(And to get the degree, of course.)* Bottom line is, this piece of paper is one of the most important pieces of paper in your life. It will pave the way to your future and allow you to be the determined, ambitious employee you've always known you could be.

I am not an expert on résumé-building. Frankly, I have always questioned if anyone really is. Every employer is looking for something different, and the truth is, the amount of time they spend looking over your résumé is sadly not very long. My advice to you is have as many people look at your résumé as you can. And I don't mean your friends or siblings, but rather people who know what employers are looking for. If you are close with your boss and they work for a big company, get advice from them. Take your résumé to your professors and campus staff at the career center. Get as much input as you can and be flexible about editing it, because again, you'll need to change and edit it according to what job you are applying for. Do not—and this is the most important part—do *not* just wing it from a template you found online.

Get the résumé-building help you need so that when you are applying for jobs, you are not wasting your time. Take this piece of paper seriously and spend a lot of time revising it. Just writing down your qualifications on a piece of paper will not get you your dream job. You need to take advice from multiple qualified professionals and ensure that you are making the necessary adjustments to your résumé.

Job Applications

Depending on where you are in your senior year, it may be time to start filling out job applications. Finding a job you could see yourself doing and applying for it should not be something you do in a couple of minutes—instead of half-assing a bunch of applications, pick a few and take your time on them. Write detailed cover letters explaining why you are a perfect fit for the job. Make sure all of your information is correct and answer their questions in a detailed manner. They are looking for applicants who are spending time on applying to work for them. Make sure you are not blowing off these applications! Make your last four years of college worth talking about.

After you submit your application, send the employer a follow-up email and make sure they received it. If you don't hear back in some time—say, a week or so—send another email. Make sure you are making yourself stand out. This is the culmination of everything you have worked for!

Interviews

Even though interviewing may come along after you graduate, it's worth preparing for it now. Job interviews are often terrifying, but the more prepared you are for these, the less scary they become. Know what to expect and how to answer each of the employer's basic questions. Attending a mock interview with one of your campus resources is a great way to stay on the ball. You can also utilize your online resources to see if anyone else interviewed with the same company and has reported what the interview was like. Do your research and try not to panic that much.

If you show the interviewer that you are committed and determined and will absolutely try your best at all times, you will do fine. Ask questions and make it clear that you are interested in their company. You want them to know how badly you want the position without directly saying it. Make it a point to remind them how important this opportunity is to you. Also remember that they are learning about who you are and assessing if you will be a right fit for their company, so do not go into this interview acting like someone completely different. Chances are if you do that, the job will not be the right one for you, anyway, and you do not want to end up at a company that has completely different values than you do even if they pay well.

You are learning about the company just as much as they are learning about you. Be respectful, curious, and assertive without stepping on their toes. Ultimately, they are looking for someone capable enough to complete the job, so show them *you* are the person they have been looking for. Most importantly, do not forget that you are a freakin' rockstar and they would be lucky to have you. You got this!

It's Okay To "Fail"

In your search for future opportunities, you are going to come across certain positions that you'll think are perfect for you, opportunities that you would love to pursue. You can't wait to send in your application! Hopefully everything will go as planned and you *will* get that job of your dreams. However, it is important to remember that even if you don't, you'll find something else you absolutely love.

There will be times throughout college when you will try your hardest and not get what you wanted. It is okay to "fail." You need to know that "failing" isn't actually "failing"—it just means that whatever you were pursuing at the time wasn't where you were meant to be. Keep reminding yourself that you will come across something else that will be perfect for you and that you will eventually land a job you'll love.

The world is filled with opportunities! You can do anything you set your mind to *if* you do not give up at the first inconvenience. Say you have always wanted to be a veterinarian and you have finished all of your pre-reqs and are on to your next step. You find a graduate program you absolutely love...but then you don't get into that one. Apply to another one and put the rejection in your past. Overcoming these times will carry you right to where you want to be.

You also must not fear failure. You must know that failing is nothing to be ashamed of. You need to be proud of the fact that you put yourself out there and tried your hardest to get to where you want to be. If things do not work out, you must appreciate the fact that you tried. It is vital that you do not let a fear of failing get in the way of trying in the first place. In most cases, you are granted as many tries as you want to prove that you are capable. Take that experience in stride and run with it! Do not fear failing—instead, look failure dead in the face and proudly move on to the next step to reach your goal.

Grad School

At this point, you may be considering furthering your education. This is a great opportunity that will ensure a higher salary in anything you choose. Or you may get nauseous at the thought of spending another minute sitting in a classroom. That's okay, too. Whichever path you decide to choose, know that you will professionally be fine either way. If you had to pay for college yourself and wish to go to grad school but can't fathom taking out another loan, a great option is to wait for tuition reimbursement opportunities. You can work as a full-time employee at almost any university and they will pay for you to further your education with them. Although most limit the amount of credits allowed, free credits are still credits towards a graduate degree. Another option is working for a company and waiting for tuition reimbursement from them. Some companies will pay for you to get a graduate degree, and then once you've completed it, they will increase your salary.

If your dream is to get your master's or PhD, you can definitely achieve that at a reasonable cost. *But* applying to grad school is extremely involved and must not be taken lightly. The majority of schools require a certain GPA, multiple letters of recommendation, your left foot, and a hell of a lot of time. Make sure you are doing your research early on so when you are getting ready to apply, you know what to expect. And also know that there are options other than graduate school, so if your grades just don't cut it, you will professionally be fine.

A past professor of mine holds a PhD in neuroscience that she obtained from a well-known, almost-Ivy-level university. Despite her undergrad GPA not being anywhere near the required GPA, she utilized her resources and was admitted anyway. She had spent most of her undergrad working in laboratories, where she spent many extra hours fixing microscopes. Her outstanding amount of extracurricular work convinced the admissions department that she had potential to shine in their graduate program. Stay active on campus and utilize your resources—you never know where they could take you.

Gap Year

Everyone will most definitely tell you to not take a gap year. They will stress that if you take a year or more off, you will never further your education or professional goals. I am here to stress the exact opposite. (Like I said at the beginning of this book, I'll say things you'll agree with and things you won't agree with. This could be one of them.) Taking a gap year is normal and can be extremely beneficial. You have been going and going for years on end—taking a break can be mentally progressive. You may need time to reflect on your prior years, and that's completely okay.

A gap year can be used to travel, save up money, or just give yourself some time to breathe. No one but you is determining your timeline. Do not be ashamed to take a gap year! You are not in a rush, and nothing you want to eventually do will slip away from you if you take time off. If you want to further your education, you will still be able to do that after taking time off. If you want to work for a huge corporation, you will still be able to do that as well. Although you may have loan payments due in just a few short months, those can be paid off with a part-time job if need be.

Some companies may ask you why you took a year (or a few years) off. You just need to convince them that it was a productive time. If you discuss how your gap year made you a better human being professionally and socially and helped you gather your priorities, they will respect your decision. If you do any traveling within your gap year—which I hope you do—stress to your future employer that you learned about cultures abroad and you thought that was important for your personal and professional growth. Taking a few years off is nothing you should be afraid to do! We all deserve to spend some time on ourselves after being in school for as long as we all were.

Take advantage of this time! Save up money, travel, pick up a new hobby or skill, and become an even better version of yourself. And never lose your motivation to continue your path once your gap time is up.

Confidence

Confidence is not only a huge part of your senior year, it's a huge part of every single day after that. I can't stress enough how important it is to keep a confident mindset during your next few years. You have worked extremely hard while you've been in school, and you must never forget the hard work and dedication you put into college. Do not lose sight of the fact that many things you thought you weren't capable of achieving you found out were actually almost easy for you to achieve. You have shown everyone around you that you are the superstar I've been telling you you are. **You have grasped this universe in full and proven to yourself and everyone around you that you have the power to be ANYONE you wish to be.** You have spent years preparing for the inevitable universe of adulthood, and now you have almost arrived. Now is not the time to lose your confidence. Now is not the time for doubting or backing down. Now is the time to believe in yourself more than you ever have!

Now is the time to remember all the years you have spent exceeding your own expectations; now is the time to know that there is a world out there waiting for you to keep exceeding expectations. It is your time to shine, and you must fully take advantage of that. Yes, it is undoubtedly a scary time to be confident. You feel like an athlete who has trained their entire life for a professional game that is finally about to start. You are nervous and anxious and you are questioning if your training was even valid. Be confident in your growth and know that you have been preparing for this for too long to back down. Get out there and show people what you are made of! Be bold during your job applications, interviews, and everything after that. Be confident in your mature choices. Be courageous in your postgraduate endeavors. **Do not fear what is ahead—know that you are prepared for anything that comes your way.**

You Are Not Alone (Once Again)

It may seem like common sense to know that you are not the only petrified college graduate out there, but if you *are* feeling like the only tadpole in the sea, you need to remember that you are one of millions. Tons of other recent college graduates are doing exactly what you are doing day-to-day. This can make finding a job competitive and difficult, but knowing you are not the only one struggling is also a humbling feeling. You are not the only one feeling like a fish out of water. You are not the only one sweating profusely going into a job interview. You are *certainly* not the only one struggling to figure out what's next. You are all in this together! Implement a plan of survival, whether that's getting a part-time job or traveling the world or taking a second to breathe. And know that you are not alone in these frightening times.

A Timeline is Just a Suggestion

If you've made it this far in my book, hopefully you've already grasped the concept that timelines are only suggestions, but I thought it was important to remind you of this again during your senior year. Some people stress themselves out right as college ends and scramble to get a job to work their way up to their dream job … just to realize they hate what they're doing. Meanwhile, other people take five years off, travel the world, and come back and land their dream job.

It's vital that you refrain from rushing into the professional world. Remember that once you enter the professional world, you will no longer have the free time you have now. The majority of the time (and depending on what field you have chosen), you won't have summers or holidays off. You'll have to strategically use your sick days each year. You have been anticipating a breath of fresh air after four years of stress has come to an end. If you rush right into a professional career, you won't catch the break (or breath) you've been hoping for. Take your time when looking for jobs—do not settle for jobs that you know you'll hate. Know what your worth is. There is no reason for you to force yourself into a position that treats you like less of an employee just because you're a recent graduate. Take the time you need, whether it's six months or five years. Do not let society's pressure conform you into a working robot. Appreciate all this world has to offer. Learn new things and see new places.

A timeline is just a suggestion, and once again, *you* are the only person in charge of your own timeline. Take advantage of your young years and live each moment to the fullest. If you take anything away from this book, know that there is no rush in life. There is no rush to get a job, settle down, etc. Life is not a race, so slow down and look around as much as you possibly can. Take days off of social media and appreciate everything around you. Do not give in to the societal pressures around you. Do your own thing and paint your own picture.

CHAPTER 27

Turning The Page

*

ALL OF THE ADVICE ABOUT PROFESSIONAL ENDEAVORS ASIDE, make your senior year as memorable and progressive as you can and give it everything you have. Stay out later than you should and appreciate those around you. Take pictures to look back on, excel in your classes, and try not to let the stress of graduating get in the way of anything. Meditate if you need to. Spend time on yourself and always remind yourself that you will eventually do great things. (And that whenever you do those great things is up to you.) Remember that your path in life is determined by the people you know and the connections you hold onto.

Make sure all of your social media profiles are cleaned up and that you present yourself in a mature way moving forward. It's important to you present yourself as an adult everywhere you go—this will allow you to run into opportunities everywhere. You are an adult now, and you need to embrace this. Although you should stay young for as long as you can, this does not mean acting immature—

this means living out your young days while not rushing into a professional setting right away. You have sculpted yourself into an amazing human being, so show that off!

In your last few months as a college student, discover even more about yourself. Learn about who you have become and reflect on how much you've grown. Look back on old pictures and laugh at the incredible times you've had. Relearn from those moments and regard the mistakes you've experienced as having been life lessons. Know that without those mistakes, you wouldn't be sitting where you are at this moment. **You have flourished into an incredible, educated, mature human being, and this is just the beginning.**

Do not look at graduating as the end of a chapter—look at it as the beginning of a new one. Know that although you will miss the times you've had in college, you are just beginning a new era, one where you'll make even more incredible memories. Yes, you will miss the people you have been surrounded with every day, but you are just about to enter a new world of lifelong friends. This is the dawn of a fresh start, a modern time for you to learn even more about yourself. Although it may be hard right now, try not to get too upset about your college career coming to an end. Look at this as a brand-new introduction to something wonderful. You have come so far!

Believe it or not, you are bound to grow even more. You will look back at this moment right now in a few years and reflect on how much you have changed in a good way. Keep moving forward and remember all of the lessons I have passed along as you forge ahead into your adventure of adulthood. You are strong and you have an extremely eventful, marvelous life ahead of you.

It has been an honor to coach you through these last four years. My only wish is that you had an amazing time and that you've learned about yourself, you've grown, and you found college to be a little easier with my advice. When you walk across that graduation stage, I hope you thank yourself and those around you who made your journey just a little more enjoyable.

Pretty soon, your name will be called out among thousands, and you'll remember the person you were four years ago versus the person you are now. You will think of your struggles and your ability to overcome them. You will remember that this is not the end by any means—it is just the very beginning. The book of adventures you have written about your own journey for the past four years has been a rollercoaster of events. **It is now time to flip the page and begin the next chapter of your adventures in this infinite universe.**

ACKNOWLEDGMENTS

I owe the successes of this book to my editor and coach, Lisa Howard. Thank you for believing in me and spending so much of your time helping me make my dreams come true. Going into this whole project I was expecting an editor to make the appropriate changes to my writing. Lisa, you went above and beyond, and were with me every step of the way. For this, I consider you my coach, as well as my exceptional editor. You gave me the confidence to flourish as the writer I always knew I could be. I would also like to thank my boyfriend, Zach Deasey. Writing my first book was not easy, you encouraged me every single day. I could not have made it through the hardest times without your support. Lastly, I would like to thank both my cover designer, Mary Ann Smith and my interior designer, Iram Allam. You have both assisted in making my dream come to life and have done a beautiful job.

Made in the USA
Middletown, DE
25 October 2022

13523555R00109